C_{T_S}

*Volumes in the New
Church's Teaching Series*

The Anglican Vision
James E. Griffiss

Opening the Bible
Roger Ferlo

Engaging the Word
Michael Johnston

The Practice of Prayer
Margaret Guenther

Living with History
Fredrica Harris Thompsett

Early Christian Traditions
Rebecca Lyman

Opening the Prayer Book
Jeffrey Lee

Mysteries of Faith
Mark McIntosh

Ethics After Easter
Stephen Holmgren

Christian Social Witness
Harold Lewis

Horizons of Mission
Titus L. Presler

A Theology of Worship
Louis Weil

Ethics After Easter

The New
Church's Teaching Series,
Volume 9

Ethics
After
Easter

Stephen Holmgren

COWLEY PUBLICATIONS
Cambridge, Massachusetts

The title *The Church's Teaching Series* is used by permission of the Domestic and Foreign Missionary Society. Use of the series title does not constitute the Society's endorsement of the content of the work.

Published in the United States of America by Cowley Publications, a division of the Society of St. John the Evangelist. No portion of this book may be reproduced, stored in or introduced into a retrieval system, or transmitted, in any form or by any means—including photocopying—without the prior written permission of Cowley Publications, except in the case of brief quotations embedded in critical articles and reviews.

Library of Congress Cataloging-in-Publication Data:
Holmgren, Stephen, 1956–
    Ethics after Easter / Stephen Holmgren.
        p. cm.— (The new church's teaching series; v. 9)
    Includes bibliographical references.
    ISBN 1-56101-176-2 (alk. paper)
    1. Christian ethics—Anglican authors. 2. Anglican
Communion—Doctrines. 3. Episcopal Church—Doctrines. I. Title.
II. Series.
BJ1251 .H59 2000
241'.043—dc21   00-025335

Cynthia Shattuck, editor; Annie Kammerer, copyeditor; Vicki Black, designer.
Cover art: *Red-Green and Violet-Yellow Rhythms*, Paul Klee

Scripture quotations are taken from *The New Revised Standard Version* of the Bible, © 1989, by the Division of Christian Education of the National Council of the Churches of Christ in the United States of America. Used by permission.

This book was printed by Transcontinental Printing in Canada on recycled, acid-free paper.

Cowley Publications
907 Massachusetts Avenue • Cambridge, Massachusetts 02139
800-225-1534 • www.cowley.org

Table of Contents

The New Church's Teaching Series

A lmost fifty years ago a series for the Episcopal Church called The Church's Teaching was launched with the publication of Robert Dentan's *The Holy Scriptures* in 1949. Again in the 1970s the church commissioned another church's teaching series for the next generation of Anglicans. Originally the series was part of an effort to give the growing postwar churches a sense of Anglican identity: what Anglicans share with the larger Christian community and what makes them distinctive within it. During that seemingly more tranquil era it may have been easier to reach a consensus and to speak authoritatively. Now, at the beginning of the twenty-first century, consensus and authority are more difficult; there is considerably more diversity of belief and practice within the churches today, and more people than ever who have never been introduced to the church at all.

The books in this new teaching series for the Episcopal Church attempt to encourage and respond to the times and to the challenges that will usher out the old century and bring in the new. This new series differs from the previous two in significant ways: it has no official status, claims no special authority,

speaks in a personal voice, and comes not out of committees but from scholars and pastors meeting and
talking informally together. It assumes a different
readership: adults who are not "cradle Anglicans," but
who come from other religious traditions or from no
tradition at all, and who want to know what
Anglicanism has to offer.

As the series editor I want to thank E. Allen Kelley,
former president of Morehouse Publishing, for initial-
ly inviting me to bring together a group of teachers
and pastors who could write with learning and conviction about their faith. I am grateful both to him
and to Morehouse for participating in the early development of the series.

Since those initial conversations there have been
changes in the series itself, but its basic purpose has
remained: to explore the themes of the Christian life
through Holy Scripture, historical and contemporary
theology, worship, spirituality, and social witness. It
is our hope that all readers, Anglicans and otherwise,
will find the books an aid in their continuing growth
into Christ.

James E. Griffiss
Series Editor

Acknowledgments

I owe a debt of gratitude to those from whom I have learned and to those who helped me in a variety of ways. First, I wish to thank my brothers and sisters who are the clergy and people of the Diocese of West Tennessee, with whom it has been my joy to serve. The first seeds of this book were sown in courses I taught there at St. Mary's Cathedral and St. John's Church, through the invitation of Frank Cooper and Jim Coleman; and with our diaconal candidates, through the invitation of our first Bishop, Alex Dickson, who did so much to encourage and help me to serve the church through my study of moral theology.

I would also like to thank the parishes and dioceses that played an instrumental role in the formation of this book by hosting me for teaching weekends and conferences where this material was presented. The thoughtful responses, comments, and questions I received during these events have had a very beneficial shaping effect on the book's content. In particular, I extend warm thanks (in order of my visits) to John Ashby and the clergy of the Diocese of Western Kansas; Arthur Kephart and the people of All Saints Church, Appleton, Wisconsin; Terence Kelshaw and the diaconal candidates and clergy of the Diocese of the Rio Grande; Larry Smith and the people of Trinity

Church, Wauwatosa, Wisconsin; Jeffrey Lee, and the people of St. Christopher's Church, River Hills, Wisconsin; Michael Anderson and the people of Holy Nativity, Clarendon Hills, Illinois; Wallace Ohl and the clergy of the Diocese of Northwest Texas; Fred Robinson and the people of Church of the Redeemer, Sarasota, Florida; John Lipscomb and the clergy of the Diocese of Southwest Florida; George Sumner, Jim Adams, and the people of Holy Trinity and St. Peter's Churches, Geneva, New York; John Gibbs and the people of St. Paul's Church, Bellingham, Washington; Dale Coleman and the people of Holy Faith, Santa Fe, New Mexico; and Jim Nutter and the people of Palmer Memorial Church, Houston, Texas. In addition, I would like to thank my students who have given me valuable feedback concerning this material in the years of my seminary teaching.

Writing this book was made possible with the grant of a sabbatical leave by the Trustees of Nashotah House, and by a grant from the Yerkes Fund at the seminary. In addition, grants from the Connant Fund of the Episcopal Church, and the Episcopal Evangelical Education Society enabled me to take a year-long sabbatical leave in order to complete this project. To these generous benefactors I am very grateful.

I owe great thanks to four persons who, in turn, have taught me to ask the questions that have shaped the vision underlying this book: Richard "Nick" Fleck, Northfield Mt. Hermon School; John Feneley, Centre for Medieval and Renaissance Studies, Oxford; Geoffrey Rowell, Bishop in Europe and formerly of Oxford University; and Oliver O'Donovan, Oxford University. To Oliver O'Donovan—who as Regius Professor of Moral and Pastoral Theology supervised my doctoral research—I owe the most, for helping me to hone my moral vision, and for the beneficial way that his teaching has influenced my approach in this book. The debt to one's teachers is never fully repaid.

I would like to thank James Griffiss for the invitation to write this book. I am also indebted to Cynthia Shattuck, Vicki Black, and Annie Kammerer at Cowley Publications for their inspired editorial and production work, and their encouragement in helping me to craft this contribution to the New Church's Teaching Series. Their work is an important form of ministry.

I would like to acknowledge the benefit I have received from sharing ideas with my colleagues Ralph McMichael and Charles Miller. Thanks also to David Cunningham for reading parts of the manuscript and offering helpful suggestions. In addition, I am grateful for help with fact-checking by my faculty assistant Mark Stevenson.

Finally, I would like to dedicate this book to my wife Martha and our sons Per, Anders, and Hans, who lovingly provide a daily community in the Body of Christ in which I continue to learn about ethics after Easter.

Chapter One

The Walk From the Font

Almighty and everlasting God, who in the Paschal mystery established the new covenant of reconciliation: Grant that all who have been reborn into the fellowship of Christ's Body may show forth in their lives what they profess by their faith; through Jesus Christ our Lord, who lives and reigns with you and the Holy Spirit, one God, for ever and ever.[1]

On an autumn Sunday in Memphis, a young woman in her thirties enters a large Episcopal church in an older neighborhood. The greeters do not recognize her and they ask if she is a visitor. In the process of introducing her to others later at the coffee hour, the greeters learn more about her. After years of inactivity, she is looking for a church home, a place to come to some maturity in the faith that is just beginning to take root again in her life. She identifies one question that she says sums up all her questions: "What should I believe *now?*" The young woman is encouraged to join an adult group that is exploring this very question on a year-round basis, a class in adult Christian formation. When she attends their next meeting, she discerns that other newcomers share her question. In turn, the explorations of this group have had an impact on the entire congregation, prompting other adult members in the parish to ask a related question, with an ancient answer: "What do we believe?"

About six months go by, during which she attends worship, reflects on her participation in the parish community, and prays and studies with the formation group. The young woman now feels that she is ready to reembrace publicly the faith once claimed on her behalf in a baptism shortly after her birth. She goes with a group of fellow parishioners down to the beautiful cathedral for the Ascension Day service. Gathered there are many candidates for baptism, reaffirmation of baptismal vows, and confirmation.

On several occasions in the preceding months she has talked with others in her group about the responsibilities that her new act of public affirmation might bring. Yet the focus of attention has been upon the basic matters of Christian belief and worship. They have been questions like these: Who was Jesus? Who is Jesus? What does the doctrine of the Trinity really mean? Why do we celebrate the eucharist every Sunday?

Now, after her reaffirmation of her baptismal vows, she finds that her focus is shifting to another question: "How should I live now?" With the other candidates from her parish who were baptized or confirmed, she begins to explore the implications of her baptism for her everyday life. The group discovers once again that they are not alone in asking this question. The members of the congregation around them are prompted to ask themselves, "How should *we* live now?"

∿ The Baptismal Question

Christian ethics, like Christian spirituality, is primarily concerned with this question of how we should live. My goal in this book is to help you think about this question as a moral theologian. This may sound loftier than it really is. Anglicans like to quote Evagrius, a Christian from the early centuries of our era, who said that someone who prays is a theologian, and a theologian is someone who prays. Thinking about the prayer that you live is the same as thinking about the faith that you live.

By what prayer and faith do you live? To what gospel do you witness by your life and work? These provocative questions are suggested by the action of baptism, which leads to other actions. Thinking about action is practical thinking, a central part of doing ethics. In turn, action is always rooted in principle, whether we are aware of it or not. This book is intended to help you be more effective in thinking about the principles that shape your daily practice as a Christian living in this world.

Our faith is an Easter faith. Our lives, therefore, ought to be Easter lives. That is why Christian ethics may also be called "ethics after Easter." Christian life begins with baptism, or with the act of resurrection-faith that comes to fruit in Christian baptism. Christian living is baptismal living, and the ethics of Christian living are "Easter ethics." In the Anglican tradition, as in the broader Catholic tradition of life and thought, Christian ethics is also called moral theology. In this book both terms will be used interchangeably.

Christian moral theology is centered on a particular vision, the vision of God. How we view our relationship with God, and God's involvement in our lives, begins to provide a focus for how we view ourselves, and what we will do. The vision of God is therefore also the vision of our humanity restored and renewed by a decisive act of God. This decisive act is God's one continuous act of being born as one of us, living in our midst while serving and teaching us, dying for us on the hard wood of the cross, and rising again in a resurrection that triumphed over the powers of evil, sin, and death. This resurrection transforms not only us, but also the whole order of the world, back to its intended pattern in creation, and toward its final end in the fulfillment of all things in Christ at the end of the ages. Among the things that are renewed and transformed by God's work of redemption is the world of human action. Christian moral theology seeks to describe this renewed and transformed world of action.

In a book that stands at the forefront of the twentieth-century revival of Anglican moral theology, *The Vision of God*, Kenneth Kirk presents in a few words the significance of this vision for our ethics: "The doctrine 'the end of life is the vision of God' has ... been interpreted by Christian thought at its best as implying in practice that the highest prerogative of the Christian, in this life as well as hereafter, is the activity of *worship*; and that nowhere except in this activity" will we find the key to our ethical problems. For Kirk, the duty of "the Christian moralist" is to stimulate in us the spirit of worship rather than set before us codes of conduct.[2]

And so we begin with a vision of God, of the order of creation and our part within it, and of God's love in raising us up to new being. The early Christian bishop Irenaeus has a particularly memorable phrase that expresses this truth: "The glory of God is the human person fully alive, and the life of the person is the vision of God."[3] Our vision of God and of what God has done for us prompts a response from within us.

We are moved to respond to God's saving acts in our life, and to ask, with the young woman in Memphis, how shall I live now? And with that same woman and her friends in the formation group, a renewed and vibrant sense of the nearness of God and of God's saving power may prompt us to pray daily these words:

> Give us such an awareness of your mercies, that with truly thankful hearts we may show forth your praise, not only with our lips, but in our lives, by giving up our selves to your service, and by walking before you in holiness and righteousness all our days. (BCP 101, 125)

Christian ethics is therefore connected with salvation, in itself a statement that we must carefully explain and qualify. Christian ethics is a primary aspect of our response to God's great saving actions on our behalf. Like spirituality, ethics is one way in which salvation takes root in our lives. In making this point we must distinguish between two connected aspects of salvation that we tend to experience as separate: *justification*, which is God's act of setting us right in relation with God, and *sanctification*, which refers to our growth into the fuller reality of that act. It is essential that we consider Christian ethics, along with spirituality, under the heading of sanctification, not justification, so that we do not find ourselves heading down the road into "works-righteousness." Throughout time, Christians have often been tempted to think that God will save them because they are good or act well. We can help ourselves to avoid this problem if we think of justification as God's act of salvation, and sanctification as our God-enabled response. Christian ethics and spirituality are therefore ways that we respond to the justification that God has made freely available to us. Seeing ethics in this way will help us to avoid the error of thinking that somehow our good works are winning us favor with God. It will also help us to distinguish what may be called "saving knowledge" from "moral knowledge." Having moral knowledge does not save us.

For Christians, ethics and spirituality are two inseparable sides of the same coin. A number of prayers that are familiar to us in *The Book of Common Prayer* express this understanding. In Morning Prayer, for example, we might offer a prayer for missions that begins with these words: "Almighty and everlasting God, by whose Spirit the whole body of your faithful people is governed and sanctified" (BCP 100). This is also a collect "for all Christians in their vocation" (BCP 256). In words that express the connection between ethics and spirituality, we pray that God's faithful people may be both "governed" and "sanctified" by the one Spirit.

Enabled by the Spirit, our ethics are the means by which we govern our actions, and our spirituality is the means by which we grow into the presence and reality of God. The General Thanksgiving from Morning and Evening Prayer, prayed by generations of Anglicans over the centuries, articulates this same connection between ethics and spirituality. In words we have already quoted, we pray that we might be moved to show our thanks to God not only with our lips in worship, but in our daily lives as well. We pray that we might give up ourselves to our Lord's service, particularly by walking before God "in holiness and righteousness" all our days. We desire that our hearts will be pure and holy—this is the dimension of spirituality. We also ask that our paths will be characterized by righteousness, which is a matter taken up in the field of ethics.

And so in these two familiar prayers we find an expression of the inseparable connection between ethics and spirituality. We need to remember this because Christian moral theology can sometimes appear to be merely an intellectual exercise. Yet we cannot accept such a conclusion for long because God in Jesus Christ has not only revealed to us moral knowledge to guide us in seeking righteousness, but has also made it clear that he desires a personal response involving our hearts, minds, souls, and bodies. Therefore when Christians think about moral theology, we will be engaged in a process that involves our hearts as well as our minds, and our lives of prayer as well as our reasoning.

∽ Baptism and the Moral Life

This connection between ethics and spirituality is clear to the young woman we have met from Memphis. As someone whose baptismal covenant is fresh on her mind and alive in her heart, she speaks of wanting to live as God would have her live and choose as God would have her choose. She has just committed herself publicly to continue "in the apostles' teaching and fellowship, in the breaking of bread, and in the prayers" (BCP 304). She is eager to know more about what that will mean in practice, and to experience its connection with the prayers.

Like her, we may find that we want to come to a fresh sense ourselves, to know what it means for our spirituality and our ethics to be knit together. Let's try to step into her shoes. For many of us, this may mean coming to look at ethics in a new light. Our questions will no longer be framed in terms of "What will God allow?" or "What is permitted?" Our questions will now have a different focus. We will find ourselves wanting to know, "How does God want us to live into our baptism?" We will wish to discover what it means to walk in holiness and righteousness here and now, in this or that situation. We will begin to realize that the questions posed in the baptismal covenant do not have a restricted focus, or a limited applicability. When I say that "I will, with God's help, proclaim by word and example the Good News of God in Christ," I am saying more than that I will tell others about Jesus, or that I will avoid public scandal. I am also saying that even in private deeds, what I do is part of a larger pattern of response to the Incarnation of God in a human person.

Ethics and spirituality have this in common: each is how we live out in our daily lives our response to the saving reality of God in Jesus Christ. The epistle to the Colossians uses the metaphor of removing our clothes for baptism to convey the significance of this great change we have made in our lives: "You have stripped off the old self with its practices and have clothed yourselves with the new self" (3:10). I remember the alarm in the eyes of a woman in my parish when she heard that the earliest candidates for baptism stripped off their clothes in preparation; she was afraid that the Episcopal Church would ask the same of herself and her two children!

What is not so apparent to us is that we are asked to do something even more dramatic and difficult. We are to leave off the old ways of living that flow from the dying world around us, and put on the new virtues of patience, meekness, and humility, like the white gown of the newly baptized. Christian ethics and Christian spirituality are both about the new human person in Christ—the Christ who comes to live in each one of us. For after baptism it is not I, but Christ who lives in me, as Paul wrote in Galatians 2:20. The New Testament gives us a vision of this new person in Christ, and prayer is the quiet and reflective way we grow into that new person. Ethics is our way of living into the reality of that new person through everyday action. Making this distinction does not, of course, preclude a genuine fusion of the two in daily Christian life. The letter to the Colossians is succinct about this new reality:

> So if you have been raised with Christ, seek the things that are above, where Christ is, seated at the right hand of God. Set your minds on things that are above, not on things that are on earth, for you have died [in baptism], and your life is hidden with Christ in God. (3:1-3)

Newcomers' classes in many of our parishes tend to emphasize new concepts or beliefs that will be a part of our life within Anglicanism, but we are often less successful in communicating that our baptismal identity has consequences for daily living. It is a powerful thing to learn that Christian converts in the early centuries stripped off their clothes for baptism in an act symbolizing a great change in their lives. Many of them literally walked away from occupations and careers because they came to perceive how incompatible those ways of living were with their new life in Christ. When the author of Colossians challenges us to separate ourselves after baptism from certain behaviors, he is not alone in the Christian tradition. As a result of "being clothed with a new self," we are to expect a renewal in knowledge and a change in our pattern of life.

> Put to death, therefore, whatever in you is earthly: fornication, impurity, passion, evil desire, and greed (which is idolatry). . . . These are the ways you also once followed, when you

were living that life. But now you must get rid
of all such things—anger, wrath, malice, slan-
der, and abusive language from your mouth.
Do not lie to one another, seeing that you have
stripped off the old self with its practices and
have clothed yourself with the new self, which
is being renewed in knowledge according to the
image of its creator. (3:5-10)

The main point is that baptism brings with it a
new self, a new life, and a new orientation that should
also bring new behavior. This understanding is clearly reflected in the prayers appointed for use in the
order for the Burial of the Dead, where we pray "that
all who have been baptized into Christ's death and
resurrection may die to sin and rise to newness of life"
(BCP 480). These words are followed by a petition to
God for all of us who are still on our journey from the
font, "that thy Holy Spirit may lead us in holiness and
righteousness all our days" (BCP 481).

We are to separate ourselves, after baptism, from
aspects of our old life. And we are to *put on Christ*, like
the new white garment with which we often clothe
infants after their "christening," following ancient
practice. We can notice in the Epistle to the Colssians
a feature that is present in many of Paul's letters—
what we might call a "hinge" in the argument. The
writer makes a transition from setting forth various
aspects of Christian teaching to delivering moral
exhortation. The apostolic witness is shared with the
expectation that lives will then change. Like other
writings in the New Testament, Colossians makes
clear what sort of features this new life will have:

As God's chosen ones, holy and beloved, clothe
yourselves with compassion, kindness, humility,
meekness, and patience. Bear with one another,

forgive each other, just as the Lord has forgiven you, so you must also forgive. Above all, clothe yourselves with love, which binds everything together in perfect harmony. (Colossians 3:12-14; see also Ephesians 4:1-5, 20)

These words can stir us to consider if there is a clear correlation in our lives between what we believe and how we live.

∼ Moral Theology and Pastoral Care
Theologians like Kenneth Kirk can help us recognize that at the heart of Christian ethics is a vision of the new person in Christ. Christian ethics is our common task of seeking to articulate and live out that vision, for as a church we shape our moral theology as a process of community reflection. Because this shaping process has a vision at its heart, and because it involves a community of real people, it can (of course) go wrong. It is never neat and tidy. We may go through periods where we do not see especially well. Or we may forget which way to look in order to be able to see clearly. This process of shaping a moral vision also needs to be distinguished from how we shape our approaches to both community discipline and community care. Moral theology is a different enterprise from church administration and governance. It is also a different enterprise from pastoral care, though of course these things should never be rigorously separated. We need to distinguish these activities without dividing them, in order to preserve the integrity of these important aspects of community life.

Most of us, for example, can think of pastoral care "horror stories," usually involving the newly ordained. Someone concerned about a pastoral situation approaches a priest after the Sunday parish eucharist, asking for some private conversation. After sharing a story with many details and complicating factors, the parishioner is disappointed. Why? Because he or she hears the priest quickly give a prescriptive response, the kind that says, "Go and do such and such." The priest may offer some time-tested rules or principles from the Christian tradition as if they provided a formula for solving the problem. Parishioners in such a situation go away confused and hurt, believing that they have not really been heard or cared for. This sort of experience results from dissolving pastoral care into moral theology, at the expense of both disciplines.

By contrast, moral theology can also be dissolved into pastoral care, with equally problematic results. For example, in our struggle to address questions in the area of human sexuality or economics, we could decide to hold a series of forums. Our goal might be to hear from people who feel that they are living on the periphery of the Christian community because of how they experience church teaching in relation to these areas of human life. We may be so moved by those whose journey has led them to feel marginalized that we try to reshape our vision of a redeemed human sexuality, or of a redeemed political economy, only in terms of their experience. In doing so, however, we risk creating the impression that we have ignored the voices of scripture and the broader Christian tradition. Then we are heading down the path of collapsing moral theology into the practice of pastoral care, attentive only to what is given in the moment. Yet the Christian community needs both disciplines, and it needs both of them to be practiced with integrity.

Let us consider an example that involves a common issue in moral theology, where we can illustrate some

of the differences between the practice of ethics and
that of pastoral care. Christians since the death of
Jesus have struggled with the question of how we
should respond to acts of violence, and whether it is
ever right for us to be involved in them. Here is a typical question in moral theology: Is it appropriate for
church members to enlist in military service? Note
that exploring this question in broad and general
terms in a study group is very different from responding pastorally to someone who is actually wrestling
with it—perhaps an eighteen-year-old high school
graduate who, pondering questions of conscience,
asks her priest for guidance concerning a decision to
enlist. The questions that are asked in both contexts
will be similar, yet obviously *how* they are asked will
be quite different. "What should *I* do now, here in
these *particular* circumstances?" is very different from
asking what *someone* should do in an unspecified
generic situation. We will explore some of the differences between these varying ways of dealing with ethical decisions later in this book. For now, let's simply
notice that asking "What should *I* do?" is more man-
ageable when we can learn from other Christians who
have spent time, energy, and prayer reflecting on the
generic question, "What should *someone* do?"

What is common to moral theology and pastoral
care is our need to discern general moral principles,
and our need to attend to particular circumstances.
Moral theology and pastoral care differ in the way
that they proceed. Pastoral care, in order to be pastoral, needs to begin with the here and now. It is most
effective when it begins by attending to the particular
situation of this person, who is sharing this particular
concern or problem, involving these particular details.
As we know from our own experience, pastoral care
that does not give priority to the particularity, detail,

and uniqueness of persons and their situations will simply not be pastoral. By the same token, moral theology needs to begin with generic features or principles. In order to provide general teaching and guidance for general circumstances, it needs to be general or generic in its scope.

In other words, Christian ethics is first of all an effort to describe the ethics of Christianity rather than of particular Christians. As a corporate process of shaping a vision for a community, our moral theology will be strongest when it aims at comprehensiveness: what has been generally true about human life and action over the course of time and across the boundaries of culture and society. As we may need to rediscover, moral theology that does not give priority to what is common, shared, and universal risks being the arbitrary reflection of our own aspirations and circumstances. Instead, it needs to be a source of guidance and a reliable reference point to help us interpret the circumstances of our actions and life.

Moral theology and pastoral care are interdependent and should never be separated, even while we try to distinguish between them. Moral theology begins with general and given principles and goes on to apply them to the specific and particular; pastoral care begins with the here and now of particular situations and moves from there toward generic principles as we seek insight and guidance. Our moral theology and pastoral care, when we do them well, should encircle one another like the two curving strands of the DNA helix, yet each having its own integrity and direction. And spirituality, or our experience of the presence of God, should be the infusing spark of energy within each activity.

Church discipline and governance are other areas of our Christian life that we often confuse with moral theology. Our approach to community discipline and governance will function best when it is informed by our principles of moral theology, but the ongoing challenge of articulating our moral vision must not be confused with implementing those principles in rules and statutory norms for community life, such as in canons. Institutional structures like the General Convention do not create moral theology, just as they do not create spirituality or doctrine. However, along with the work of individual moral theologians, the General Convention should seek to *articulate* our moral theology, giving it voice and contemporary expression. We can see how this occurs when we examine the various study reports that are produced for consideration by each General Convention. Material from these Blue Books often goes on to become the source of canons and resolutions that are passed by the Convention. Clearly, as the church engages in this process of seeking to give our moral principles faithful expression in these canons and res- olutions, we are just as likely to fail as to succeed.

~ The City of God

A living sense of the risen Christ in our midst is essen- tial to articulating our moral vision. If the spirit of the risen Christ does not rule in our hearts and minds, then a lesser spirit will rule at the center of our being. St. Augustine, in his mighty work entitled *City of God*, describes the difference between that "city" and the "city" of this world. The City of God is the communi- ty of those who love God to the contempt of self; the city of this world is composed of those who love self to the contempt of God.[4] The City of God expresses what we can call a "theocentric" understanding of the world, where God is at the center of reality. The other city stands for an "anthropocentric" understanding of the world, where you or I see ourselves as being at the center. One reflects the order of creation before the fall; the other reflects the disorder of the world after it.

The Easter mystery presents us with a challenge. Will we die to self and to a life without God, so that we might rise with Christ and live unto the glory of God? Or, forsaking that glory, will we rise to self and die to the abundant and nourishing opportunities for growth and renewal that the Lord seeks to provide? Happily, we are not unclear about the appropriate answer to these questions. Each member of the Christian community has already answered them at least once, and perhaps many times. With God's grace, we stand and give the answer in our baptismal covenant. With that same grace, we will stand and have the opportunity to reaffirm it many times hence. As a reminder of the power of these questions, and their place in our ethics and spirituality, we should make it a practice to reaffirm our baptismal covenant on a regular basis. By doing so, we develop our awareness of how Christians over the centuries have tended to answer the very ancient question: How shall we live now?

The baptismal covenant presumes a connection between the content of our faith and the nature of our response to it. Together as a community, both the candidates for baptism and all others present, we are invited to renew our covenant and confess our faith in God and in God's saving acts, through our recitation of the Apostles' Creed in dialogue form. Then the celebrant asks questions of everyone present that draw out the implications of sharing this faith as members of the One Body:

Will you continue in the apostles' teaching and fellowship, in the breaking of bread, and in the prayers?

Will you persevere in resisting evil, and, whenever you fall into sin, repent and return to the Lord?

Will you proclaim by word and example the Good News of God in Christ?

Will you seek and serve Christ in all persons, loving your neighbor as yourself?

Will you strive for justice and peace among all people, and respect the dignity of every human being? (BCP 304-5)

We can find in these words the basis for a whole program of Christian ethics for the Christian community. It is important to stress that these questions point us to the truth not because they are in the prayer book, but because they express and embody a vision of post-baptismal Christian life thoroughly grounded in the scriptures. These questions point us toward the truth that the decision for Christian baptism is not simply a decision to affirm and make one's own a particular pattern of religious belief; it is also a decision to affirm and make one's own a particular pattern of religious living. Moral theology concerns itself not only with this pattern of religious living, but also with the close interrelationship between it and the pattern of Christian faith.

As Christians, our life has a new focus: we live through the grace of God toward God, under God, through God, and in God, in the mystery of the Holy Trinity into which we are incorporated by baptism. From there we are sent forward by God into the world to do the work that we have been given to do, offering and rededicating ourselves to God. We walk forward into those good works that God has provided for us to walk in as a response to the redemption that God has freely worked on our behalf. Like spirituality, Christian ethics is part of our response to the gospel, not a means of securing some aspect of our redemption. We are sent forward with a positive vision, shored up by the exhortation "Walk in love as Christ loved us," in the Spirit.

What then is the Christian life according to moral theology? The authors of a contemporary book have put it well:

> Christian life is not primarily the following of a moral code. It is, most fundamentally, living as adopted sons and daughters of God. This new life is made possible by the redemptive activity of Jesus. It essentially involves *participating in God's own life*, in living freely in ways that God's grace makes possible. This grace is God's altogether free gift.[5]

Their statement captures a central insight from the apostle Paul. At the end of a passage that is very important for Christian moral theology he writes, "If we live by the Spirit, let us also be guided by the Spirit" (Galatians 5:25). The Spirit who is our counselor, the one through whom Jesus continues to be with us, is the Spirit that we should seek as the guide for all our decisions and actions. The reality of God is our reality—the trinitarian reality in which we "live and move and have our being." Our tendency is to think of the life of Christian freedom primarily in terms of what it is freedom *from*, whether from sin and death or from the law. Our moral theology may well be fuller if we focus our attention on what this freedom is *for*. Yes, we have been set free from our ancient enemy—whether we think of this as the Egypt of Satan, sin, death, or human enemies—but as with the people of Israel, God has also delivered us unto a new land, that we might serve him "without fear, holy and righteous in his sight all the days of our life." For God has come among us "to guide our feet into the way of peace" (BCP 92-93). Our challenge now is to try and describe some of the features of this walk in Christ, and some of the resources we have for reflecting on it.

∿ Axioms for Moral Theology

At the end of each chapter, I will provide a summary of some of the key points we have explored in the form of axioms for Anglican moral theology. Axioms are basic principles that are widely accepted as a basis for further thinking and reasoning together. They provide a foundation upon which we can build our moral theology.

1. Moral theology is about a life of holiness. After baptism, we seek to walk "in holiness and righteousness all our days." In moral theology we seek to describe and commend a life worthy of our calling. (This axiom is the foundation of all the rest.)

2. Moral theology is properly considered under the heading of sanctification, not justification. It is part of our walk from the font. Doing good will not save us; we do the good because we have been saved.

3. Moral theology is not the same thing as, but is intimately related to, pastoral care. Moral theology begins with the consideration of generic principles; pastoral care begins with the consideration of a particular situation.

4. Church conventions and other legislative gatherings do not "make" the church's moral theology. Instead, they face the challenge of applying its moral principles to community legislation and discipline.

Chapter Two

Seeking to Live a Good Life

> *Grant to us, Lord, we pray, the spirit to think and do always those things that are right, that we, who cannot exist without you, may by you be enabled to live according to your will; through Jesus Christ our Lord, who lives and reigns with you and the Holy Spirit, one God, for ever and ever. (BCP 232)*

On a quiet evening in Advent, words from a familiar hymn can surprise us with newly found power: "Cast away the works of darkness, O ye children of the day." Or while pondering the glory of the Epiphany, another hymn can give voice to an unexpected resolve welling up within us: "I want to walk as a child of the light. I want to follow Jesus."[1] In these moments of spiritual insight we recognize how much room we have for conversion and growth, especially when it comes to *living* our faith. In the familiar words of St. Richard of Chichester:

> Day by day, dear Lord, of thee three things I pray:
> to see thee more clearly, love thee more dearly, follow thee more nearly, day by day.[2]

Yet how shall we follow our Lord more nearly, in all our acts and choices? What does Christian ethics have to do with this?

∾ What are Ethics?

We can start with a relatively simple description. Ethics are theories about right action or permissible conduct. We use them both to guide particular acts and to shape the whole course of our lives. There may be many times on any given day where we find our-selves acting spontaneously, making choices on impulse. Yet we also know that we can think, reflect, and pray about what we have done and about what we plan to do. Because ethics is primarily concerned with thought about action, ethics involves what is often called practical reason. We engage in practical reason when we think about what we will do (or have done), and about how we will act (or have acted). In the process, we are usually influenced by a variety of considerations that may not appear to be directly rel-evant to the action that we are contemplating. This is especially true for religious persons. As Christians, we are called to shape our acts and our lives with refer-ence to a broad understanding of the world, its origin and true end, and our place within God's purposes for it. In other words, we believe that the meaning of our actions should be connected with what we come to know about the meaning of life.[3]

Non-religious ethics, and the ethics of other reli-gious traditions, also make reference to the purpose, meaning, or value of human action in the world. For example, in most of our communities there is a serv-ice organization called Rotary International, which has an interest in business and community ethics. "Rotary ethics" can then be described as theories about how we should act in business and community life that are in keeping with the aims and ideals of Rotary. Many places of work also have codes of ethics that are oriented to the good of customer service, or to the greater good of the company. To take an example from world religions, Buddhist ethics involves thinking about right action in ways that conform to the life and teachings of the Buddha as well as to the tradition of reflection based upon them. Jewish ethics consists of theories about how we should live and act that are in keeping with the law, the prophets, and the writings as well as the rabbinical tradition. In the same way, Christian ethics is thinking about right action in ways that are shaped with reference to the moral good that we know in and through Jesus Christ. It is oriented to the Christian scriptures and to the Spirit-guided tradition of reasoned reflection based upon Jesus' incarnation, life and teaching, death and resurrection.

Having said that this is the case about Christian ethics, we have not yet said what it *means* in terms of ideas, principles, or rules. We will need to ask, what is the "moral good" that we know in Jesus Christ? Matthew's gospel records several sayings of Jesus that seem to speak directly to this point. A young person asks him, "Teacher, what good deed must I do to have eternal life?" Jesus responds with his own question, "Why do you ask me about what is good? There is only one who is good. If you wish to enter into life, keep the commandments" (19:16-17). In the first part of his response, Jesus does not challenge the young man's assumption that pursuing the good in this life is linked with entrance into the next. Jesus also confirms the link between the moral good and keeping the commandments.

In a similar story told by Matthew, Jesus responds to a question with words that are now a familiar part of the prayer book. A Pharisee lawyer tests him by asking which commandment in the law is the greatest. Jesus says,

> "You shall love the Lord your God with all your heart, and with all your soul, and with all your mind." This is the greatest and the first commandment. And a second is like it: "You shall love your neighbor as yourself." On these two commandments hang all the law and the prophets. (22:37-40)[4]

Jesus' words here are often referred to as the Love Command. The command has two aspects: a proper love for God, and a proper love for neighbor. These in turn correspond to the two halves of the Ten Commandments, also called the tables of the law, which these words summarize.[5] Visitors to English churches will often find the two tables of the law painted on the walls on either side of the chancel for the purpose of Christian education. Jesus tells us that his command to love not only sums up the Ten Commandments but also captures the essence of all of the law and the prophets, two of the principal parts of the Hebrew Bible. Paul tells us something similar in Romans 13:8-10, when he says that love of neighbor sums up the other commandments that concern our relations with other persons. A third saying of Jesus recorded by Matthew provides a more general parallel: "In everything do to others as you would have them do to you; for this is the law and the prophets" (7:12).

Jesus' answers to the questions that are put to him might help us to ask a question of ourselves: Why do we wish to identify the moral good? Do we want to discern the moral good mainly so that we can find out what is permitted? Or do we want to identify it so that we can learn what God asks of us? The first question tends to encourage a habit of thought unfriendly to good theology and ethics. This is the habit of reductionism, of reducing the scope and power of any idea to one of its components. If we ask only about what is permitted, we head toward an ethical minimalism and a moral theology that is detached from worship and spirituality. This is like the adolescent who is only interested in what he or she is *allowed* to do on the weekend. Looking at free time in this way prevents us from considering things that might be valuable to do, like extra reading or volunteering to help coach an elementary school basketball team.

The second question, which inquires about God's will for us, prompts us to look at a wider horizon. This question is more likely to remind us of a truth that we affirm in baptism. We live and act in a creation whose center is the living God, rather than in ourselves and our own proud wills. One collect inspired by Paul begins, "Heavenly Father, in you we live and move and have our being" (BCP 100). In these words that remind us how all of life depends on the enabling presence of God, we can see some of the moral power contained in the Genesis 1 and 2 creation accounts. In a creation that is ordered and contains moral value, and where a fruit tree at the center of the garden symbolizes the divine will, the first man and woman displace God's will by asserting their own. Ever since the fall, human beings have struggled to remember to ask, and to answer openly and honestly with their lives, a profound question. It is the question we ask as we walk from the font: What does God ask of us? How should we live, in light of the Easter mystery?

~ Two Views of Ethics

The two ways described above to answer the question "Why we want to discern the moral good?" correspond to two ways of seeing Christian ethics. The first way, which focuses on what is required and what is allowed, tends to see ethics along the lines of human civil law. Laws that govern everyday life, such as those concerning traffic regulations, the payment of taxes, or conduct in relation to other persons, usually articulate certain minimum standards without which society cannot function effectively. These standards are often framed in terms of what can practically be enforced, such as speed limits. If we see moral theology or Christian ethics in these terms, we will have a concept of guidance for the Christian life that tends to be based on minimum requirements, enforcement, and discipline. We can see how this is true when we expand the question "What is allowed?" to include "by the church." Our focus shifts to institutional requirements and the possibility of sanction.

The second way of answering the question corresponds to a different approach to moral theology. If we start with reflection on what God asks of *us*, we are more likely to think in terms of ideals or goals that challenge us to reach higher and do more. We will tend to think of our moral principles more in terms of the Beatitudes and Jesus' teaching in the Sermon on the Mount, and less in terms of a code of requirements and prohibitions. To observe this is not in any way to denigrate the laws, canons, and rules that are needed for community governance and discipline. It is only to distinguish the purpose and content of moral theology from the purpose and content of civil or statutory law. We will explore this distinction further below.

People often ask, "Isn't Christian ethics basically about love?" This sensible question might prompt us to wonder if the familiar song refrain isn't correct, that "all you need is love." After all, Jesus tells us the Love Command sums up not only all the other commandments but also much of the teaching of the Hebrew Bible. So it is true that Christian ethics is basically about love, yet Jesus' observation can help us notice an important point. As a primary principle for Christian ethics, love is never a minimal starting point but a *comprehensive* starting point. If we ask what love means or what love involves, as we respond to other persons and to common situations in daily life, we discover the wisdom in Jesus' words. Love involves all the other commandments. We can agree that "all you need is love," but if we stop to think about it, this is saying a lot.

This awareness can lead us to a further question. Suppose we grant that Christ-like love will be the moral good that will shape our notions about right action. And suppose we grant that Christian love includes the meaning of the Ten Commandments. Does that mean that we can build a complete approach to Christian ethics upon the Ten Commandments? As with many questions in this area of Christian theology, it helps to resist the impulse to answer with a simple yes or no. Our moral reflection upon living a life worthy of our calling may well be shaped by the full meaning of the Ten Commandments, but it may also be shaped by other principles. Here we need to reflect a little bit more on something that we can observe everyday. It is easy to notice how fellow church members or neighbors who do not share common principles in their ethics can readily disagree with one another. Yet we can also notice that persons who identify the *same* good or principles as the foundation for their ethics may nevertheless understand that good in very different ways.

Why is this? Often it has something to do with the source of our principles.

～ Where Do We Find the Good?

The answer to this question comes from a surprising source: the theory of law.[6] Have you ever wondered where law comes from? It turns out that asking where we find the moral good is a lot like asking where law comes from. Many people like to say that we find our concept of the good in the structure of the world and in the nature of human persons. This is often called the *natural law* approach, which claims that certain moral principles are given to us through nature, both in our experience of being human and in our experience of the world around us. Those who hold this view will say that, in some important ways, morality is rooted in reality. Far from being based on our own ideas or feelings, some moral principles are "out there" and not just "in here," and we discern them through the use of reason. We encounter and apprehend some moral principles as we do other objects in the world around us; they have not been created by human communities or through human will. Yes, particular communities or cultures have understood these principles in different ways at differ- ent times, but the principles themselves are universal and timeless.

Other people like to say that we find our concept of the good in another way—through the traditions, lit- erature, and practices of our families and communi- ties. In this *historicist* view, the good is what has been continuously valued and handed down by those who have come before us. The good is what has stood the test of time. There are many ideas and practices that we retain because, as we like to say, "we have always done it this way." This view makes no claim to universality. Nevertheless, what is identified as the good in this approach does not seem abitrary because it has come to us from before our own time, and apart from our own choice.

Still other people believe that we find our concept of the good in a third way: from choices and acts of will, both our own and those of our community. The fact that something is said to be an aspect of reality (the natural law view), or that many generations have believed it before us (the historicist view), is not of first importance. Instead, a principle is of value for us because we have agreed upon it and have chosen to identify it as the good. We might decide differently tomorrow, or next year, but for now it is a shaping principle simply because we have expressed our will about it through *choice.* Of the three, this positivist approach is the most vulnerable to the charge of being arbitrary, yet it also provides the greatest measure of freedom for change and revision in light of new and better ideas.

We should recognize two points as we consider these three approaches to identifying the moral good. First, all three approaches may be wrong at any given time. Whether we rely on nature, history, or convention, all three are capable of yielding wrong or bad answers to the question, What is the good? Therefore, we may want to look at them not from the point of view of deciding which one is "right." Instead, we may want to inquire about the strengths and weaknesses of each approach when we want to correct what was previously misidentified as the good. Second, very few of us employ only one or another of these three approaches, nor do we employ them consistently. It is far more likely that we engage in ethical thinking by using more than one approach, as we do in many other areas of human thought. We may have varying reasons for making an appeal to the nature of reality, to the traditions of our community, and to the opportunities provided by convention and choice.

Sometimes two of the approaches are so intermixed in our minds that we do not stop to examine the basis of our assumptions. For example, someone might say, "People have always recognized that women are inferior to men." Another variation is, "People have always recognized that blacks are inferior to whites." One response is simply to get mad and tell the person he or she is just plain wrong. A more productive way of responding is to try to sort out how these disturbing claims rest upon an appeal to nature and to tradition, and then to examine and evaluate the evidence that appears to support them. Later in this book, we will return to the challenge of addressing similar wrong assumptions based on the approaches that stress nature, history, and convention. Here we simply want to notice the importance of understanding the differences among them.

∾ Applying the Three Approaches

We noticed earlier that people can identify the same good as a foundation for their ethics and yet understand that good in very different ways. If we wanted to use the Ten Commandments as a foundation for Christian ethics, how might we understand their role? We could start with the natural law approach and say that the Ten Commandments represent the moral good because they articulate what is true about human life in the world. Here we could focus our attention on the particular commandments that govern our relations with other persons and say they are principles that can be discerned from human experience by thoughtful people who seek the good. In other words, these commandments express something that is true about reality, whether one happens to be a Christian, a Buddhist, or a Jew. Like the natural law of which they are a part, they stand over and above us as principles not of our own making. They hold our thinking, choices, and actions to account, and provide a measure of moral value independent of our particular experience and perspective.

Even though the Bible is clearly the product of a particular people with a particular history, it is possible to approach scripture in two ways that are related to the natural law view. First, we could say that the biblical authors articulate ideas that they claim are evident to people through common experience, as the prophet Amos does in his oracle against foreign nations at the beginning of the book that bears his name.[7] (Paul makes a similar argument at the beginning of his letter to the Romans.) Second, we could understand scripture by thinking in terms of revelation. We can describe revelation as knowledge that is made available to us by God, which therefore has a source that is independent from us. It functions as a "given" aspect of reality that we encounter and respond to, just as we do objects and circumstances in the world around us. In this sense, someone can claim that the Ten Commandments are an authoritative source of and for the church's lived faith. Someone who takes this approach can still maintain it even in the knowledge that the early Christians, through a long process of prayer, reflection, and discussion, determined which texts were and were not scripture. He or she can say that scripture was recognized as revelation by the early church in the same way that the principles of natural law are discerned. In both cases, the object of attention has a source of authority beyond the particularity of time, community, and tradition.

We can also appeal to the historicist approach in our understanding of how the Ten Commandments provide our notion of the moral good. According to this view the commandments, whether in full or in the summary form articulated by Jesus, are the received texts of our people and our tradition. Their continuous use and transmission to succeeding generations hallow them for us. They are texts and principles that have exercised an authoritative role in our community, shaping its life and guiding its members over the ages and in a myriad of circumstances. We can still speak in terms of revelation, but here the evidence for revelation is the fact that the biblical texts have been validated by centuries of use in worship and in doctrine. In this sense, someone can claim that the Ten Commandments are an authoritative source in the church's lived faith. Here the source of authority is located primarily within the life of the community over the course of time.

A third way of understanding how the Ten Commandments are a source of the moral good involves the positivist approach, which appeals to convention. It is our act of choice that makes these principles authoritative for our individual and common life. Our incorporation of them in our worship and education materials makes them the good that will shape our thinking about what is right ethical action. According to this view, someone can claim that the Ten Commandments are made an authoritative source by the church's lived faith. Once again, the source of authority is located within the life of the community, but here the emphasis is placed upon the present moment and our acts of choice.

As we have observed, each of these approaches is capable of being wrong. The most common example is the way natural law has been used at certain points in history in support of the institution of slavery. Another frequently cited error involves the historicist approach. Many medieval Christians, influenced by Aristotle, believed that the charging of interest on loans was morally wrong. In both cases, the false thinking of prior generations was corrected by an appeal to what can be observed from the nature of reality: the true dignity of human beings and the true nature of money. In other words, natural law was used to correct bad natural law thinking in one case and an over-reliance on traditional thinking in the other.

These examples can help us to recognize that the misuse of a concept like natural law does not necessarily invalidate it for other uses. We often appeal to a more proper understanding of the created order of the world as the best antidote to false understanding. As we shall see in the next chapter, for example, natural law has been used to support a deeper respect for human rights and the conservation of nature.

Our concept of the good plays a primary role in shaping our thinking about right action, because it includes assumptions about the purpose and meaning of human life. In this regard, Christian ethics has two primary reference points that provide the foundation for all subsequent thinking about human action and the task of shaping a godly life. These two reference points are creation and the Bible, traditionally called the Book of Nature and the Book of Scripture. Moral theology, when pursued in a full way, will appeal to the order, structure, and beauty of God's creation, and to our experience of it and of each other within creation. It will also appeal to scripture and the tradition of reasoned reflection that has been based upon and shaped by the Bible. It has been consistently recognized within Anglicanism as well as the fuller

Christian tradition that both sources are avenues of God's revelation to us. That does not mean that they are equivalent in terms of their significance, their content, or their accessibility, but only that they have a common source and may serve a common purpose. In chapters three and four we will discuss how each of these sources serve as a reference point for moral theology.

This leads us to another axiom for Anglican moral theology. There are two primary sources for our moral principles: creation and scripture. Some true moral principles are learned through creation and through our experience of life together in the world, while others are derived from the Bible and the basic structure of Christian doctrine. Scripture and Christian doctrine play a fundamental role in shaping moral theology. Once again, having said that this is the case about moral theology is not yet to have said what precisely this means. It is only to identify clearly some of our initial reference points.

∾ The Role of Salvation History

At this point, you might well want to ask, "What about the fall? What about its marring effect upon the order of creation, and upon our ability to perceive or understand it?" Important questions like these lead us to reflect on the way Christian doctrine shapes Christian ethics. When we pray the eucharistic prayers, when we recite the creeds or sing the *Te Deum*, we remind ourselves of an important context in which we understand our relationship with God: salvation history, the history of God's relationship with creation. Four principal phases, or "moments," make up salvation history: creation, fall, redemption, and the end of all things. We speak first of God's creation of all things and of time. We next acknowledge the fall of humankind by sin, and the resulting distortion of the created order. Third, we proclaim God's work of redemption. Here we focus on the preparation for, and completion of, God's incarnation in the life, death, and resurrection of Jesus. And finally, we anticipate the end of all things and of time in Christ: the _eschaton_, from the Greek word meaning the end. This history provides the basic structure of Christian doctrine. It also gives a basic shape to Christian ethics or moral theology. Much in the same way that the human body shapes the garments in which it is clad, these four moments of salvation history provide a fundamental shape for our ethics.

At the center of our moral theology is the call to live a holy and good life, a God-centered life rather than a me-centered life. As we search to know how we should live in light of the Easter mystery, our questions will be shaped by salvation history. What kinds of acts, and what ways of living, reflect God's ordering of the world in creation? How are our actions colored by the distortions of sin and the fall? How are these actions embraced, transformed, or set aside for some higher good through God's work of redemption? Finally, how do our acts stand in relation to what we know of God's final purposes for us and for the creation at the end of time? All these questions arise from the habit of making reference to salvation history in our approach to moral theology.

We might want to say, for example, that openness and directness in speaking with one another is a divinely intended feature of the order of creation. Friendship and honesty could therefore be described as "goods" that are part of the order of creation. Yet we would quickly have to acknowledge that none of us experiences these or other goods—work, marriage, sexuality—in the way that they were originally intended. Furthermore, daily experience reminds us that friendship can often bring pain as well as enhance life, while human speech is often characterized by deceit, as when we are being "economical with the truth"! Clearly, human sin has distorted these goods of creation so that we experience them sometimes as a mixed blessing. What about God's purposes for friendship and honesty in redemption? How have God's saving initiatives through the life, death, and resurrection of Jesus Christ transformed and restored creation from its fallen state? Do we have any evidence that these goods of creation are consistent with God's purposes in redemption, and will they have a continuing reality in our new life of fellowship around the throne of the Lamb?

If we ask these same questions about medicine and private property, we can see how important they really are. We can do this by making reference to the creation narratives in Genesis, providing that we are not overly literal with the texts. Was private property an original feature of the order of creation? Clearly not, for all things in the Garden of Eden were created to reflect the divine glory and to be shared for the benefit of all human life. The same is true of medicine. Neither medicine nor illness would have been features of the good order of creation; both private property and medicine are features of human life that arose after the fall. The key question is this: did these two features of human life arise from human sin, or are they gifts of God for human life that temper the effects of the fall? The great medieval theologian Thomas Aquinas, who did much to shape the future of moral theology, saw private property as a gift of this latter sort. Following his example, we can say that both medicine and private property are features of human life that have arisen since the fall but are consistent with God's redemptive purposes.

Clearly there are other aspects of human life that we will evaluate differently because they are neither consistent with the good order of creation nor with God's redemptive purposes for the world. Here we will identify aspects of the world that reflect the disordering effects of sin and the fall, such as greed, exploitation, and our abuse of the gifts of creation—whether ourselves or others, animals or things. As we look at our life in the world through the lens of salvation history, the challenge is to discern which of our activities undo God's work of redemption. Which of our activities have their end in this world and which of them will find fulfillment in the hereafter?

∼ **Four Ways of Responding Pastorally and Theologically**

These reflections can help us to distinguish at least four ways that we can respond pastorally and theologically to different aspects of moral life. First, we can affirm and celebrate the goods intended by God in creation, such as friendship, marriage and sexuality, work and play. Second, we can affirm acts or patterns of living that arise after the fall but still fit in with God's purposes for creation and redemption, such as medicine and private property. Third, in our community life we can seek to make pastoral accommodation for the effects of sin upon our daily living that can be incorporated into God's continuing work of redemption. This binding of wounds might include remarriage in the church after divorce and the adoption of children. Finally, we will encounter aspects of life that are inconsistent in every way with God's work of creation and redemption: the disordered enjoyment, exploitation, or abuse of created things, including ourselves. Fraud, sexual abuse, and political torture are perhaps the most obvious examples.

The distinction between these four modes of theological and pastoral response may not always be clear in practice. There are a number of concepts central to Christian ethics where clarity at the level of principle does not preclude a measure of ambiguity in practice. Such questions are best pursued in community, and in the context of our theological tradition. As Richard Hooker observed, "The most certain token of evident goodness is, if the general persuasion of all men do so account it."[8] Anglicans place great value on consensus because it is one of the most persuasive forms of assurance we have. This is especially true when we find ourselves asking the "How do we know?" questions. For example, we can study creation's forms and patterns in search of meaning, but how do we know that a particular principle is really what the Author of the Book of Nature would have us learn from it? Within Anglicanism, consensus about the answer has generally been regarded as an important indication that we have arrived at something true.

We should notice the way Hooker makes his point concerning consensus, or what he calls the "general persuasion." He recognizes that consensus can be both greater and lesser: it is never absolute. Consensus provides us with a measure of assurance that is not the same as certainty or a guarantee. We are usually more persuaded by principles that reflect consensus among the people we respect, and more cautious when that is not the case. Clearly, consensus is not our only ground for accepting or believing in something. We want to think for ourselves, and have the opportunity to risk going against the grain of public opinion when we believe that we are right. We want to reason, and we want to be free to evaluate the resolve of an evident consensus that exists within our community. The Anglican tradition of moral reasoning respects the value of such a consensus, and the freedom that we wish to exercise in relation to it.

Some readers may be uncomfortable with the ambiguity involved in these observations. Yet we need to recognize and acknowledge an important feature of Anglicanism: Anglicans do not have an "answer book" for difficult questions in ethics. We have no single authoritative source comparable to papal encyclicals, nor do we read scripture in such a way as to find ready and unambiguous guidance for dealing with moral problems. Given that this is true, we need to build a case when we seek to respond to ethical questions, and strive to make that case persuasive by appealing to the teachings of nature, scripture, and the Christian tradition. And the more we can demonstrate that our point of view reflects a consensus, the more persuasive it is likely to be. As Anglicans, we are involved in a search for greater assurance, realizing we will never have certainty this side of the New Jerusalem.

We can now articulate two further axioms for Anglican moral theology. First, in coming to agreement about the pattern of a life that is worthy of the calling, Anglicans have looked for consensus. Second, Anglicans have looked for consensus in three inter-related spheres: the praying community of the church throughout the world, the wider community of the Body of Christ through history, and academic communities that are founded upon Christian principles.

∾ Axioms for Moral Theology

5. Moral theology has two primary reference points: creation and scripture. Moral theology

looks both to the world and our experience of life together within it, and to scripture and our tradition of reasoned reflection based upon it, as sources of moral principles.

6. Moral theology works in light of an understanding of the four principal phases of salvation history: creation, fall, redemption, and the end of all things in Christ.

7. In coming to agreement concerning the pattern of life that is worthy of the calling, Anglicans have looked for consensus. We have the greatest degree of assurance for what has been most widely received.

8. Anglicans have looked for consensus in several interrelated spheres: the praying community of the church throughout the world; the wider community of the Body of Christ through history; and the academic community, when its work is founded upon Christian principles.

Chapter Three

The Book of Nature

> *Almighty and everlasting God, you made the uni-
> verse with all its marvelous order, its atoms,
> worlds, and galaxies, and the infinite complexity
> of living creatures: Grant that, as we probe the
> mysteries of your creation, we may come to know
> you more truly, and more surely fulfill our role in
> your eternal purpose; in the name of Jesus Christ
> our Lord. (BCP 827)*

Walking out onto Mather Point or one of the other
dramatic overlooks at Grand Canyon National
Park in Arizona, it is common to hear expressions of
awe and wonder from the visitors. Confronted by the
stunning, multicolored expanse and the sheer drop of
the canyon walls, those of us who are religious believers are often moved to whisper words of praise to our
God, who has given us the evocative wonder before
us. We are not alone in our response: our sense of awe
in these moments links our experience with the
authors of the psalms, who on many occasions mar-
veled at the wondrous scale and the beauty of both
mountain and sea. "The heavens declare the glory of
God, and the firmament shows his handiwork," proclaims the writer of Psalm 19. The fact that many of
the features of our world are vast in scale, remarkably
patterned, and arrestingly beautiful has provided

grounds for generations of Christians to say that in nature we have experiential proof of the existence of God. Nature is like a book from which we can draw clues about its author.

We have seen how Christian ethics takes for one of its starting points the basic structure of Christian doctrine. This involves looking at the world and our ethics through the lens of salvation history. We assume that the structure and beauty of the world witness to the existence of the creator. But can the created order tell us of God's intentions for ethics in the human community? Do we discern moral value in the objects and actions that we experience in daily life? Two important concerns are often raised in connection with these questions, one theological and the other secular and cultural.

Let's look at the first. Suppose someone asks, "Where do Christians find their moral principles?" We may wish to say that the answer includes at least some reference to the world around us. However, some Christians believe that because of the fall and its effect on creation and human reason, human beings cannot discern God's moral will in the world without the special revelation of the Bible. Furthermore, to say that non-Christians can also perceive moral good seems to imply that saving knowledge (and even salvation) is available to everyone on the basis of natural, everyday experience and knowledge.

When we examine this concern, we can see that we need to make a distinction between *saving* knowledge and *moral* knowledge. To say that all people can discover the moral good through their experience of the world is not in any way to say that they will find saving knowledge. Let's try putting the question like this: Can we say that non-Christians are simply unable to discern any aspect of the moral good, on the basis of

their experience of life in the world? Or that they
receive no knowledge of the moral good from the traditions of their communities? If so, then we have a
hard time accounting for how non-Christians can
appear to act ethically in daily life. How could a non-
Christian in the business community, for example, act
with honesty, justice, and charity? How would such a
person come to know that it is wrong to treat others
as less than human because of their color of skin or
gender? We might concede that Jews, unlike the followers of other religions, receive true moral knowledge from the Hebrew Bible. We might also
acknowledge the parallels between Old Testament ethical teaching and aspects of the folk wisdom of other
non-Christian cultures. If so, then we are closer to
saying that non-Christians also have access to *some*
knowledge of the moral good apart from the special
revelation of the Bible or conversion to Christianity.
The most striking example is the parallel we see
between Jesus' teaching of the Golden Rule and the
ethical principles found in Buddhism and other
Eastern religions.

The second concern is raised by modern secular
culture. If moral knowledge is encountered in the
world, is the moral value really there—in the actions
we witness or in the objects we encounter? Or is it
merely something that we project outwards upon the
face of the world? In contemporary western Europe
and North America, we tend to give primacy to the
way that we filter and shape our experience rather
than to the objects that are the source of our experience. We are ever alert to all the ways in which, as
philosopher Iris Murdoch describes it, "our minds are
continually active, fabricating an anxious, unusually
self-preoccupied, often falsifying *veil* which partially
conceals the world."[1] When we do, we show that we

are heirs of the modern intellectual tradition, which encourages us to take pride in how far we have progressed from more naive ways of looking at the world.

Newspaper reports and our conversations with others seem to confirm on a daily basis this deep-rooted suspicion that many of us share. Even supposedly objective accounts of events frequently appear to us subjective; these accounts are shaped as much by those who experience and describe them as by the events themselves. For example, one witness interviewed in a news story may say that a woman lunged toward her assailant and tried to take the gun away from him. Yet another witness may firmly believe that, in her frightened surprise over the encounter, the woman simply stumbled and fell toward him. If this can be true about the facts of an event—the details gathered from eyewitnesses to a crime—how much more is it true of our *moral* evaluation of events in daily life? We may honestly come to doubt that any analysis of events can provide us with moral clarity. For example, could we ever know whether the woman in the above scenario was right to go on the offensive and try to take the gun from her attacker—if, indeed, she was trying to do so?

Knowing the extent to which we invest acts and events with our own meanings, it follows that at least some of the time moral value is our projection upon the world of our experience. The question that we must explore in this chapter concerns whether moral value is ever a given and knowable feature of the acts and events that we encounter. Another way of putting the question is this: We can agree that moral value is sometimes "made," but is it ever "found"? Or, to invert the question, can we deny that moral value is ever a given quality of the events or objects we come upon in our world? A very strong current in the Anglican tradition of theology and prayer encourages us to agree that moral value can exist independently of us in acts, objects, and events.

Iris Murdoch's approach is helpful here. Although a non-Christian philosopher who was aware of how we can project meaning and value outward onto the world, she also saw moral value as something that we find in the world. She argued against the tradition of thought, influenced by the philosopher Kant, which claims that the human will alone is the source of moral value. Instead Murdoch would like us to develop a spirit of humility in the face of the world. Although she was unable to affirm the presence of God, she writes that there are "many patterns and purposes within life." She is able to think in terms of human nature that "has certain discoverable attributes," and she suggests that these should be considered in any discussion of morality.[2]

~ Reading the Book of Nature

As we observed in the last chapter, thinkers and writers in the Christian tradition see the created world as one of two sources of knowledge and revelation. Nature is a "book" to be "read" just as scripture is. Two biblical texts, one from the Wisdom of Solomon and the other from the letter of Paul to the Romans, are especially important to this idea:

> You have arranged all things by measure and number and weight. (Wisdom 11:20)

> For what can be known about God is plain to them, because God has shown it to them. Ever since the creation of the world his eternal power and divine nature, invisible though they are,

have been understood and seen through the things he has made. (Romans 1:19-20)

For Anglicans these passages support the idea that creation is a medium of divine communication in a way that is analogous to scripture. Whereas the Book of Scripture has been seen as "special revelation," the Book of Nature has been understood as providing "general revelation." God is the "author" of both books, although this is not meant to imply that the two are comparable in significance or interchangeable. The Book of Nature provides its readers with practical and moral knowledge; the Book of Scripture adds a third and higher form of knowledge that only it can provide, which is called saving knowledge.

Consider the following texts, which provide only a brief glimpse of a large body of literature about creation. Many Episcopalians pray these words at every eucharist:

> We give thanks to you, O God, for the goodness and love which you have made known to us in creation; in the calling of Israel to be your people; in your Word spoken through the prophets; and above all in the Word made flesh, Jesus, your Son. (BCP 368)

When we pray these words, we are saying that God has revealed goodness and love to us through more than one source. God has revealed goodness and love to us in creation—not simply in the act of creating, but in everything that results. We also say that God has revealed goodness and love in the Word spoken and in the Word made flesh. The Outline of Faith, or Catechism, in *The Book of Common Prayer* shares a similar view: "God first helped us by revealing himself and his will, through nature and history, through many seers and saints, and especially through the prophets of Israel" (BCP 845). The Catechism tells us that God's own self and God's will are revealed through nature and history as well as through the prophetic tradition, whose wisdom is preserved in scripture. Eucharistic Prayer D speaks of the same idea in saying, "We acclaim you, holy Lord, glorious in power. Your mighty works reveal your wisdom and love" (BCP 373).

The collect that introduces this chapter is entitled "For Knowledge of God's Creation." The word "of" is objective and subjective: we pray for knowledge about, and knowledge gained from, God's handiwork in creating the ordered complexity of the world. The knowledge received here is not limited to reason understood as merely acts of measurement, comparison, and deductive logic. Reason is more profound: through it we explore the mystery of creation, where we encounter the divine purpose and our role within it. A number of hymns express a similar vision, such as Joseph Addison's paraphrase of Psalm 19:

> What though in solemn silence all
> move round the dark terrestrial ball?
> What though no real voice nor sound
> amid their radiant orbs be found?
>
> In reason's ear they all rejoice,
> and utter forth a glorious voice;
> for ever singing as they shine,
> "The hand that made us is divine."[3]

This same psalm, which has inspired so many writers, also prompted the text for a more contemporary hymn:

The stars declare his glory;
 the vault of heaven springs
mute witness of the Master's hand
 in all created things,
and through the silences of space
 their soundless music sings.

The dawn returns in splendor,
 the heavens burn and blaze,
the rising sun renews the race
 that measures all our days,
and writes in fire across the skies
 God's majesty and praise.

So shine the Lord's commandments
 to make the simple wise;
more sweet than honey to the taste,
 more rich than any prize,
a law of love within our hearts,
 a light before our eyes.

So order too this life of mine,
 direct it all my days;
the meditations of my heart
 be innocence and praise,
my rock, and my redeeming Lord,
 in all my words and ways.[4]

Words on this same theme from medieval Jewish liturgy are preserved in a hymn text that portrays God as speaking to us both through creation and through the Word. As with the hymn above, we should notice here how the word law is used in a broad and poetic way to refer to a pattern of order, rather than narrowly referring to statutes and prohibitions. It is also more than a coincidence that these writers convey through verse their vision of how the ordered rhythms of creation can teach our moral imagination. This educative role transcends the impoverished role that we more usually associate with law in our moral thinking. It is more typical for us to connect law with the task of constraining the will, rather than seeing law as connected with broad, even imaginative, principles. Here we sing,

> Formless, all lovely forms declare his loveliness;
> holy, no holiness of earth can his express.
> Lo, he is Lord of all. Creation speaks his praise,
> and everywhere, above, below, his will obeys.
>
> His Spirit floweth free, high surging where
>   it will:
> in prophet's word he spoke of old; he speaketh
>   still.
> Established is his law, and changeless it
>   shall stand,
> deep writ upon the human heart, on sea,
>   on land.[5]

∾ A Glorious Gospel

These ideas found in scripture, poetry, and worship texts run right through the Anglican tradition of theological reflection. Most of us have heard of the sixteenth-century divine Richard Hooker, whose great contribution to Anglican theology is his *Laws of Ecclesiastical Polity*. Hooker had a rich and nuanced view of the world and of God's providential relation with it. He challenges us to see beneath the surface of things and recognize a principle of order within creation, which provides knowledge of the moral good. Hooker wrote:

> For that which all men have at all times learned
> nature herself must needs have taught; and God
> being the author of Nature, her voice is but his
> instrument. By her from him we receive what-
> soever in such sort we learn.

Hooker continues by quoting Paul's words in Romans
2:14 about the Gentiles who unconsciously do what
God's law requires. Through reason, they learn the
moral good not by any "extraordinary means," such
as revelation, but by what Hooker calls "natural dis-
course."[6]

In other words, God provides all persons with natural avenues to moral knowledge. Moral knowledge,
in turn, provides a foundation for the higher, saving
knowledge we encounter in scripture. The gift of reason with which each of us is born leads, when applied
to ordinary experience, to a lifelong process of observing and making distinctions. Thus everyone has basic
knowledge of the good that is to some extent capable
of sorting out true from false, good from evil. The
cumulative effect of using reason and reflection in this
way is positive and wide-reaching. All persons have
an opportunity to discern the will of God and we can
articulate what we learn in the form of norms for the
human community.

The work of two nineteenth-century Anglicans
expresses an understanding of creation similar to
Hooker's. Samuel Taylor Coleridge, well known as one
of our most gifted poets, was also a religious thinker
who came to have a strongly trinitarian theology. In
"Frost At Midnight" Coleridge provides this vision of
creation as an instrument that speaks the wisdom of
a divine teacher:

> So shalt thou see and hear
> the lovely shapes and sounds intelligible

of that eternal language, which thy God
utters, who from eternity do teach
Himself in all, and all things in himself.[7]

Theologian and poet John Keble, who edited an edition
of Hooker's works that remains in print today,
expressed a similar vision. Based on themes in the les-
sons and collects appointed for Sundays in *The Book of
Common Prayer* lectionary, Keble wrote a series of
poems entitled *The Christian Year.* In his texts for the
season after the Epiphany, Keble's theme is the divine
knowledge that is available to everyone. Those of us
who associate the Epiphany too narrowly with the
revelation of light to the Gentiles in the manger, he
warns, may miss the fuller significance of the star in
the biblical story. Keble, like the bishop and preacher
Lancelot Andrewes before him, perceived that natural
wisdom can lead us to seek the Lord through whom
all things were made. In his poem for Epiphany 1
Keble wrote:

Every leaf in every nook
every wave in every brook
chanting with a solemn voice
minds us of our better choice.

In verses written for Epiphany 4 we find:

When souls of highest birth
Waste their impassioned might on
    dreams of earth
He opens nature's book
And on His Glorious Gospel bids them look
Till, by such chords as rule the choirs above
Their lawless cries are tuned to hymns
    of perfect love.[8]

Keble was known to his friends as someone who had such a high regard for the Bible that if a book was inadvertently placed on top of it, he would get up and remove it. Yet he had no hesitation about referring to the face of creation as a "glorious gospel" whose "text" is capable of bringing order to unruly lives and tuning "their lawless cries . . . to hymns of perfect love." Even if we turn our eyes away from the glory of God and pursue the things of the world for their own sake, God still provides opportunities for us to rediscover the divine purpose for our lives in the ordered patterns of this world.

This confidence in the accessibility of *some* knowledge of God and God's will for us is rooted in a high view of both the creation and the incarnation. Notice the parallel between the prologue to John's gospel and the creation story in Genesis 1. John chooses to refer to the Son of God as the Logos, the principle of reason and order. "Through him all things were made," we say in the creed, and all things stand in some relation to him. Moreover, Paul's speech in front of the Areopagus at Athens, recorded in the book of Acts, is based on a similar view of God and the world.

What therefore you worship as unknown, this I proclaim to you. The God who made the world and everything in it . . . himself gives to all mortals life and breath and all things. From one ancestor he made all nations to inhabit the whole earth, and he allotted the times of their existence and the boundaries of the places where they would live, so that they would search for God and perhaps grope for him and find him— though indeed he is not far from each one of us. (Acts 17:23-27)

Both sinners and saints, both Christians and unbelievers, have access to basic moral principles through our experience of God's creation. Anglicans as well as other Christians in the broader catholic tradition of thought have followed these themes in John's gospel and Paul's letters. Some aspects of divine wisdom, as well as God's intentions for creation, can be perceived in the structure of the world.

Interpreting the Book of Nature

Many of us have learned some words from the Declaration of Independence that are quite significant for the ideas we are exploring here. After the signers refer to the "Laws of Nature and of Nature's God" that entitle a nation to assume a new position among world powers, they declare, "We hold these truths to be self-evident, that all men are created equal, that they are endowed by their Creator with certain unalienable Rights, that among these are Life, Liberty, and the pursuit of Happiness."[9] As we have already noted, claims like these may appear problematic today if they are accepted in an uncritical way. What is the evidence for these claims? Is it assumed that all persons will, of necessity, perceive these truths? Are these "self-evident truths" always the same truths, not subject to the differences of custom and culture, time and place?

If we find ourselves asking these things, let us pause to recall the way we are exploring the central question about the sources of moral value. We take it for granted that human beings can and do invest the objects of their experience and attention with moral value. The question therefore turns on whether or not the actions or objects that we observe within human experience have inherent moral value of their own. We looked at a number of texts from Anglican worship, both hymns and prayers, which strongly suggest that

we do encounter moral value in the structure of the
world that has been bestowed by the hand of the creator.

Consider an example from outside the western tradition. Bai Young, a Chinese dissident author, published a *New York Times* editorial article in 1992 called
"The Torturers of Lingyuan." In reporting on the
appalling treatment of prisoners at a labor camp
(called a "factory") in his homeland, Mr. Young presents a grim picture that western Christian readers find
deeply disturbing.[10] The author and the companions
about whom he wrote are in all likelihood not
Christians. Yet Bai Young demonstrates the same sort
of moral repugnance toward the inhuman treatment
of prisoners that we would expect from any Christian
moral theologian. He implies that any reasonable person would agree that these acts of torture are wrong.
Why? Because they violate a fundamental principle of
order in the world: human beings should not treat
other human beings as objects, irrespective of their
status as persons. Persons, unlike objects, possess the
capacity to reason, learn, work for the good, display
emotion, and give love. Bai Young's article may help
us to recognize that these are moral principles that we
can learn by observation and reflection upon our life
in the world with other persons. We can learn them
through the experience of compassion and the exercise
of our reason whether or not we read the Bible,
because these principles are generally revealed in the
pattern of the created world.

Based on our theological sources as well as upon
our experience of creation, Anglicans put forth a claim
that corresponds to the standpoint of a writer and
thinker like Bai Young: there is a relationship between
morality and reality. Yes, we can embellish and distort
what we perceive, both in the way we think about it,
and in the way we describe it to others. Nevertheless,

our morality has its source in the reality of the creation that precedes, surrounds, and will survive us. To claim that this is the case is not yet, of course, to say in any way what that morality is. We are simply offering an observation based both upon our experience and our more central theological convictions.

One of the many compelling aspects of the creation-myth narratives in Genesis is the way that divine activity in creation is portrayed in Genesis 1, where God is described as setting the various aspects of the universe in order. This theme is echoed, as we have observed, in the prologue to John's gospel. In addition to giving each thing its own place in creation and setting it in relation to everything else, God pronounces each part of creation "good." Everything within the order of creation has a given moral value, independent of and prior to human acts of perception. In a well-known passage from Job, which is appointed for Morning Prayer on the feast of St. Michael and All Angels, God asks Job with a measure of irony,

> Where were you when I laid the foundation of the earth? Tell me, if you have understanding. Who determined its measurements—surely you know! Or who stretched the line upon it?
> ... Surely you know, for you were born then, and the number of your days is great! (Job 38:4-5, 21)

These texts remind us that our moral reflection occurs within the context of God's creation, the reality that precedes our consciousness of it. Quite simply, the world was here before we were here to notice it. Though such a statement seems obvious, today we tend to think and act as if the opposite were true. Instead, we approach circumstances and events as if they were the proverbial blank slate awaiting our acts of will and reasoning to give them their order and meaning. Twentieth-century Anglican theologians, however, have been no less interested in the created natural world than their predecessors, especially its significance as a given reference point for reflection and action. William Temple, the Archbishop of Canterbury and theologian who died in 1944, addressed this point at the beginning of his Gifford Lectures. The Gifford Lectures are a distinguished series of endowed lectures on the theme of natural theology—theology that does not rely on the "special revelation" of scripture. Temple writes that the world we apprehend existed long before we did, so that as far as our experience is concerned, "apprehension takes place within the world, not the world within apprehension."[11] Furthermore, a contemporary theologian, Keith Ward of Oxford University, makes clear the connection between the givenness of the natural and the givenness of the moral. Just as chairs and tables exist independently of us, he writes,

> so there are independently existing aspects of being which give rise to moral obligations, and which can be understood by us. Morality is not, in other words, a matter of human decision, taste, or emotion, for which there is no correct and incorrect, no understanding to be won, nor error to be avoided. In morality, as in the sciences, one can progress and learn.[12]

What ethics and the sciences have in common is this: what we observe lies beyond us and exists prior to us. It is true that quantum physics has made us aware of some ambiguity in the relationship between the observer and the observed at the level of particles. Yet without some confidence that the world of objects and actions is characterized by certain observable constants within which variability occurs, science would not be possible.[13] The same is true for ethics. Yes, we do construct meaning and order in our minds. But the world of nature possesses meanings of its own that have been placed there by the creator and precede any meanings we might want to give it. The challenge for us is to try and discern where the two diverge.

⟋ Morality and the Book of Nature

At the end of the Second World War, those involved in trying the Nazi officials of the Third Reich for war crimes had to rely on this important distinction. Suppose that all moral value is something that human communities make for themselves and for others over whom they gain power. If so, then any subsequent judgment of that moral value and the laws based on it are potentially just as arbitrary. The court at Nuremberg recognized that many of the activities for which Nazi officials were being tried did not in fact break existing German laws within the Third Reich. The court determined, however, that the crimes of the Holocaust violated something much more fundamental because these were "crimes against humanity." They violated moral principles embedded in the nature of reality and accessible to human reason regardless of whether or not particular individuals had happened to notice them or not. The crimes of the Third Reich were therefore crimes against a morality that is integral to reality.

Of course human communities can always claim that their laws are based on these kinds of moral principles. For example, many Christians in the past regarded slavery as compatible with the order of nature. Yet the most compelling way of showing that such notions are wrong is not for one group simply to claim that its own principles are better than those of others in the march of progress. Rather, by claiming that moral value is inherent to creation, we place our moral conversation under a discipline. We must then reason together in the awareness that our understanding of moral value is always subject to comparison with the reality that our claims are supposed to describe. We know that we will encounter false claims about moral principles, and to set these aside we will need to demonstrate through reason how these inadequate principles fall short of and are judged by the actual order of the world. Comparison makes correction possible.

As a way of illustrating this point, let us consider the case of Aung San Suu Kyi, a human rights activist in Myanmar, formerly known as Burma, and winner of the Nobel Peace Prize. On what grounds could a concerned Christian from the United States make an appeal to the government of a Communist country with a Buddhist cultural tradition? Let us recall from the last chapter the three principal ways of accounting for our concept of the good. Suppose that, on behalf of Aung San Suu Kyi and her husband, we make an appeal based on western traditions of concern for human rights. And suppose we also appeal to our long-standing religious and philosophical belief in a high degree of individual liberty. Representatives of the Myanmar government could respond to this historicist argument by saying that it is well and good for us to have such beliefs. They could say that we should follow such beliefs in our own countries so that our approach to life will have integrity. On the other hand, they could prefer to follow the deep-rooted cultural patterns of their own country and tradition by choosing to put the apparent good of the community before that of certain individuals.

If we find that the historicist approach fails, we could try the positivist approach and go on to appeal to the United Nations Universal Declaration Concerning Human Rights. Here we could say that the nations of the world, irrespective of their particular cultural traditions, have jointly agreed upon certain minimal standards that should be observed in the treatment of prisoners and political detainees. This approach would seem to allow a broader range of appeal than an historicist approach that is dependent upon the history and tradition of particular cultures. Yet representatives of the Myanmar government could still refuse to honor our concerns by saying that their present government never signed this United Nations declaration. Furthermore, even if they had done so years ago, they are now free to change their minds and no longer view it as binding upon their internal political life.

The third approach assumes that our concept of the good is located in the structure of reality rather than in the traditions of particular communities or common acts of will. We could argue, therefore, that it is contrary to universal aspects of human nature and human community to treat human beings in certain ways. Here the Myanmar government could continue to resist our appeal by saying that we have fooled ourselves into thinking that we share a common humanity that underlies our differences of culture and customs. Yet this argument would turn on whether or not our assumptions actually fit with the nature of the world. Thus we could try to show how denying the existence of a common humanity can be a dangerous starting point for international relations and for participants in a world economy. The overall point here is that no approach is assured of success in advance. Yet in this situation, the third approach provides the broadest opportunity for an appeal to reason and human experience because it assumes a given structure of moral value that is inherent in nature.

In the course of this chapter we have seen how the Anglican tradition has consistently upheld the natural created order as a reference point for moral and religious knowledge. The Book of Nature complements the Book of Scripture in providing all people with a way to acquire moral principles. This is not to claim that all people will take the opportunity to pursue moral knowledge, nor that everyone who does will do a good job of discerning and articulating those principles. In making a case for a fuller understanding of our doctrine of creation we must, of course, give proper attention to the implications of the fall. However, there is a central question that we must ask, whether from a theological vantage point or not. Shall we entirely exclude from our ethics the idea that ordinary persons can, in their experience of and reflection upon human action, discern aspects of the true moral good? Far from excluding this idea, we have seen from this brief look at our tradition how Anglicanism encourages us to be open to the ways that God teaches us moral principles through our experience of and reflection upon creation.

~ Axioms for Moral Theology

9. All people, whether they are Christian or not, can receive moral knowledge through the "general revelation" of the Book of Nature. This is not to say that all people will do so, or that they will choose to act on such knowledge.

Chapter Four

The Book of Scripture

Almighty God, you have given your only Son to be for us a sacrifice for sin, and also an example of godly life: Give us grace to receive thankfully the fruits of his redeeming work, and to follow daily in the blessed steps of his most holy life; through Jesus Christ your Son our Lord, who lives and reigns with you and the Holy Spirit, one God, now and for ever. (BCP 232)

A film was released a few years ago about a boy who finds a magical object lodged in the ground, marred and covered with dirt from not being touched for years. What turns out to be an old box captures his imagination, and when he takes it home and opens it up, a whole new world unexpectedly emerges. The boy comes to see that this object has the power not only to transport marvels from another world, but also to take him to that other world. If you or I were to encounter that box with all its dangerous possibilities, we might prefer to leave it alone. But the boy takes the risk, and the box changes his life in ways he could never have imagined.

You may recognize the scenes described above from the film *Jumangi.* The story seems far-fetched in many respects, but there is one way in which every one of us can identify with it. Somewhere in our own homes, most of us have an object with similarly unexpected power that often remains unexplored. And for many of us, it may be in a condition similar to the Jumangi game when the boy found it: dusty from not being touched for years, and probably tucked away somewhere, out of sight. This thing with the power to make present another world is the Bible, and it has the power to transport us to another world. Yet we too, like the characters in the movie, are tempted to put it away somewhere, and forget about it. It has too much potential to destabilize our lives and our world. Worse yet, many of us have forgotten the power this book has, and so our neglect of it is based on boredom or indifference, rather than fear. We have forgotten the power of this strange gift.

In a letter that St. Paul wrote to Timothy, he urged his coworker to

> continue in what you have learned and firmly believed,....how from childhood you have known the sacred writings that are able to instruct you for salvation through faith in Christ Jesus. All scripture is inspired by God and is useful for teaching, for reproof, for correction, and for training in righteousness, so that everyone who belongs to God may be proficient, equipped for every good work. (2 Timothy 3:14-17).

These are challenging words. Paul is saying that an object which we have sitting up on a shelf somewhere is actually God-inspired. Furthermore, it is intended for our growth in righteousness so that we may be prepared for ministry. How do we respond to these words? The challenge is made harder because of the greater knowledge and increased awareness that we have gained from modern biblical studies. We know, for example, that by the word "scripture" Paul meant the Hebrew Bible, our Old Testament, and he probably never imagined that in a short while the very letter in which he wrote those words would itself be seen as part of scripture. In addition, the same biblical scholars would caution us against being too sure that Paul actually wrote 2 Timothy, given certain identifiable features in the text. We have come to know things like this through our study of the Bible, and this kind of investigation has taught us much that is of value. But it also creates a danger. Something happens when the Bible becomes an object of formal study. When we approach the Bible in the way that an historian approaches the letters of Napoleon, for example, we distance ourselves from it. The Bible becomes a detached object of attention, like cells on a glass slide under a microscope. We become judges of what we see. Yet if God still speaks to us through the Bible, and if it does contain words of correction and instruction for us, then we have to be open to a different way of seeing it. We have to be open to letting the Bible also become the measure for us.

A metaphor from the ancient Greek poet Homer helps to express the challenge that we face in trying to learn from scripture as we shape our moral theology. Based on some of the imagery in his epic poem, *The Odyssey*, we can talk about the challenge of sailing a vessel between Scylla and Charybdis—between a hard rock on one side and a whirlpool on the other. Though these hazards radically differ, both obstacles can impair the journey. Anglicans usually try to steer a course between running into a "hard" literalism in their reading of scripture, and being sucked into a whirling skepticism where everything dependable seems to get lost. A more positive way of describing this challenge is to say we want to steer a course that allows us to affirm something of value in two differing positions. Nevertheless, an image from scripture will chasten us about the danger of relying on the middle course itself. In the Apocalypse of John we hear the message from "the one like the Son of Man" to Laodicea. He says, "I know your works; you are neither cold nor hot. . . . So, because you are luke-warm, and neither cold nor hot, I am about to spit you out of my mouth" (Revelation 3:15-16). How do we proceed?

Since the time of the first followers of Jesus, Christians have had a preeminent regard for scripture as the instrument of God's own voice. Our tradition recognizes that it is a mark of mature piety to stand before scripture in a posture of humility—the same posture that Iris Murdoch urges us to adopt before the natural world. At the same time, our tradition has encouraged us to take seriously our membership in Christ's body of believers, which cautions against clinging too closely to what may simply be a private interpretation of the Bible. Occasionally we need to put some distance between our insights about the meaning of these texts and ourselves, testing our own perception against the understanding of the wider Christian community. As the Catechism reminds us, "We understand the meaning of the Bible by the help of the Holy Spirit, who guides the Church in the true interpretation of the Scriptures" (BCP 853-54). You may notice another parallel here: the challenge is very similar to that of shaping moral theology with the Book of Nature. Testing our own reading of scripture against its interpretation by others makes correction possible.

This need for correction is a principal reason why Christians turn to the Book of Scripture as well as the Book of Nature. Though there are many things that we can learn from our encounter with the world around us, it will not teach us about salvation. From the earliest days of the church Christians have believed that the Book of Scripture, as well as the wider context of liturgy and teaching in which it is read, provide a vision of reality that we cannot obtain by our own efforts and energy: a divine view of the world and our place within it.[1]

The Anglican reading of scripture is as much a corporate activity, shaped by history and disciplined by consensus, as an individual one. When speaking about scripture as a source for Christian moral principles I find it best to use an extended phrase: scripture and the tradition of reasoned reflection based upon and shaped by it. As Anglicans, we read scripture in the context of what the creeds and the Catechism call the "one, holy, catholic, and apostolic" church, a community with a very long and significant tradition of reflection. We also read scripture in the context of Christian doctrine and worship, products as well as shapers of our tradition. As we have noted, to emphasize this point is not to discourage an appreciation for Christian freedom, a theme we will explore further below. It is only to mark some of the important features of the terrain in which the exercise of Christian freedom occurs.

∼ **The Distinctiveness of Christian Ethics**
We need to reflect a little bit further on a theme we have already introduced on the relationship between our two sources for moral principles. We can affirm both creation and the Bible as sources of revealed moral principles without saying that the two sources are equal in their significance, or that *moral* knowledge is the same as *saving* knowledge. We also saw that because of the fall, Christians will be cautious about claiming that all persons who *can* receive moral

knowledge from creation will do so. The effects of the fall are still in evidence in our world, despite God's ongoing work of redemption, begun in the incarnation, life, death, and resurrection of our Lord. Nevertheless, we cannot rule out the possibility of non-Christians deriving true moral principles from their experience of life in the world.

That said, it is still possible to describe how Christian ethics might differ from those of other faiths or no faith. The simplest way to articulate what is distinctive about the Christian approach to the moral life is this: Jesus makes a difference for ethics. A whole new pattern of special revelation, building upon that of the Hebrew Bible, is focused on the person, ministry, death, and resurrection of Jesus Christ. Our ethics are therefore transformed and enhanced when they are shaped with reference to Christian scripture, doctrine, and the reality of baptism.

There are two primary ways that we can express this difference. First, the Jesus we meet in scripture makes a difference in shaping our ethics. Followers of Jesus hear his words, remember and imitate his acts, and witness to the redemptive power of his cross and resurrection. Second, the Jesus in whom we live in the church also makes a difference in shaping our ethics. Being in Christ prompts us to seek the mind of the risen Christ in all that we do, we who have been joined with him in his death and resurrection. We live in him, he lives in us, and we have received the gift of the promised Spirit. For the sake of intellectual clarity we need to distinguish between the Jesus that we meet in scripture and the Christ in whom we live, but we should make sure that we do not separate concepts that belong together.[2] A collect from the order for Evening Prayer reflects the way in which these ideas belong together:

Lord Jesus, stay with us, for evening is at hand
and the day is past; be our companion in the
way, kindle our hearts, and awaken hope, that
we may know you as you are revealed in
Scripture and the breaking of bread. Grant this
for the sake of your love. (BCP 124)

∾ The Jesus We Meet in Scripture

The first way of describing the distinctiveness of
Christian ethics has three aspects. The Jesus we meet
in scripture is significant for our ethics because of his
teaching, his own moral example, and his role as
mediator. What he tells us to do or not do, how he
himself lived and responded to circumstances, and
how he has acted on our behalf are all reference points
for Christian ethics. Jesus functions as mediator when
he acts on our behalf in circumstances that do not
necessarily provide a direct moral example for us. For
example, Jesus died on the cross for our sins, not so
that we might literally imitate his example. It is sometimes hard to tell how a passage in scripture is best
understood: Is Jesus presented as a moral exemplar, or
is he acting on our behalf? A good example is the
cleansing of the temple in John's gospel, which is of
interest to those who are trying to build a case for, as
well against, Christian participation in acts of violence
under specific circumstances.

In addition to the way that Jesus makes a difference to moral theology as teacher, exemplar, and
mediator, there is a second way to describe the distinctiveness of Christian ethics. The Jesus in whom we
live in the church also makes a difference to us as we
live our lives and reflect on our acts. Put most directly,
Christian ethics differs from other ethics in this way:
we are in Christ, and we have received assurance that

our approach to the moral life is God-enabled, Christ indwelled, and Spirit led. We cannot presume either that this is so in our own case or that it is not so for others; we can simply give thanks for the promises and assurance that we have received as Christians. Ethics after Easter is an ethic that reflects the mystery of our incorporation into the death and resurrection of our Lord. We live in the same world of moral action as everyone else, yet who we are as moral agents will be transformed by and accountable to a new reality: if anyone is in Christ, he or she is a new creation.

In this chapter we will explore the distinctiveness of Christian ethics with regard to the Book of Scripture, addressing some of the issues raised for moral theology by the person of Jesus, his teaching and example, as well as by the church's ongoing experience of the Risen Christ and the leading of the Holy Spirit. An overview of biblical ethics is not possible within the scope of this book, for two reasons. The first is simply a matter of scale: the space we have available will allow us to mention only a limited number of topics without extensive examples from the biblical text. Second, a more expansive account of the biblical material would duplicate other fine studies of biblical ethics already in print.[3]

Before we proceed, I want to make a preliminary point. A substantial number of lay and ordained Christians since the eighteeenth century have treated Christianity and the Bible as if the primary value of our faith lay in the moral improvement that it can provide. This trend has often been associated with a decline of interest in the supernatural aspects of our religion. We have already noted the problem of reductionism—more specifically, the problem of reducing ethics to the task of shaping community rules and legislation. A similar problem on a greater scale arises when we reduce the significance of Christianity to the ethics that it inspires. This would be to overlook the important link St. Paul makes in his letters: God has saved you; therefore, live as someone whom God has freely saved! These transitions from doctrinal exposition to moral exhortation link two mutually dependent areas of meaning. This is the connection between faith and action that the epistle of James also tries to make clear, and reflects the pattern of covenant expectations that was placed upon Israel after the Exodus, evident particularly in Deuteronomy and echoed in the prophets.

The content of our faith has implications for our lives; at the same time, how we live reflects a faith. Easter does not simply add an article to the creeds; we are called to let Easter shape all our days. We do not read the Bible simply to glean ethical principles; we read the Bible as a way of opening ourselves to respond ethically to the "things necessary to salvation" we find there.[4] The practical effect of this insight can surprise us. The way that we live every day proclaims a gospel to our neighbors. What gospel do they "read" when they see how we live and act, and the choices that we make?

∾ Following the Jesus We Meet in Scripture

If you look closely at the bracelets or necklaces worn by some folks at church, particularly those in the youth group, you may notice four letters: WWJD. These letters are a shorthand reference to the question, What would Jesus do? It has become popular to commend this question to Christians as a way of helping them to make choices in everyday life. Though some of us may not like the religious jewelry on which this logo is found, or the way in which items bearing these letters are marketed, we need to embrace the question. Like all good questions, its value transcends the answers it sometimes gets.

The New Testament, and a good bit of the Christian tradition as well, presents Jesus as a moral exemplar for the faithful. As in the title of a much-loved medieval mystical text, Christians in all ages have found themselves drawn to "the imitation of Christ." Though he bids potential disciples to follow him, Jesus only indirectly commands us to follow his own moral example. "Love one another as I have loved you" comes closest. Yet the value of his own example is implied in his teaching. On what basis could he criticize the Pharisees for hypocrisy if he were not above the charge himself? Our mental picture of Jesus assumes that he attended to "the weightier matters of the law: justice and mercy and faith," unlike the pharisaic preoccupation with "mint, dill, and cummin" (Matthew 23:23).

We find great power in the Beatitudes and the Sermon on the Mount because we find in these words a Jesus who must have embodied every precept. Scholar Servais Pinckaers notes how St. Augustine found in these words the epitome of the moral life.[5] When we hear Jesus say that he has not come to abolish the law and the prophets, but that he is concerned about its every stroke of the pen, a stark choice remains. Either the Jesus of Matthew is a wonderfully integrated being in whom teaching and action perfectly coincide, or he is a hypocritical charlatan who masquerades as something he is not. Convinced that the former is true, a strong Christian piety has moved many believers since the first followers of Jesus to try to approximate something of this integration in their daily lives. This is why we so often find ourselves asking, when confronted by a moral challenge, "What would Jesus do?"

As we can see, the New Testament presentation of the teaching of Jesus clearly provides a reference point for Christian moral reflection. Biblical scholars often point out the contrast between the Beatitudes as we find them in Matthew and Luke, particularly the difference between Matthew's "Blessed are those who thirst *for righteousness*" and Luke's more simple "those who thirst." The Sermon on the Mount in Matthew emphasizes not only the importance of righteous conduct, but also purity of heart as the inward source of upright conduct: anger or lust in the heart is just as problematic as anger or lust manifested in outward acts. Another distinctive feature in Matthew's presentation of Jesus' role as teacher is the parallel between Moses' transmission of God's law at Sinai, and Jesus' teaching and embodiment of the new "law" on the Mount. Paul also develops this parallel by contrasting the fading reflected glory of God's presence on Moses' face as he descended the mountain with the unfading glory we see in the face of Jesus Christ.

Ethicists are often drawn to Matthew's presentation of the teaching of Jesus, but they find Luke's gospel to be an equally compelling source. For example, Luke's concern for the poor is evident in his presentation of the Beatitudes: "Blessed are the poor" instead of Matthew's "poor in spirit." Luke alone presents Jesus' conversation with the man in the crowd who asks him to convince a brother to divide a family inheritance (12:13-21). In his response, Jesus strongly cautions against greed and reliance upon worldly wealth, and then tells the memorable parable about the man who sought to secure the future by building large storehouses. Many stories in Luke's gospel, moreover, complement this emphasis by portraying significant compassion for those in need. What may be one of the most loved of Jesus' parables, that of the Good Samaritan, is found only in Luke and expresses this compassion most profoundly by making the point that neighbors are those who act in a neighborly way.

What about the differences between Matthew and Mark, which by comparison seems to preserve so little teaching from Jesus? And what shall we say about John? In asking these questions, we are touching upon what is called the synoptic problem and the question of identifying a possible "canon within the canon." The first three gospels parallel one another in some striking ways, in terms of structure and content. They present a *syn-optic*—or parallel—view of Jesus, whereas John's view of Jesus and his teaching is so different that it raises the question of which should take precedence. As we try to shape a moral outlook, shall we privilege some parts of the New Testament over others? For example, do we give priority to the synoptic gospels, or to the moral world view of Paul's letters, which were largely written before the gospels? These are the sorts of questions we will find ourselves asking as we begin to read the Bible with an effort to discern moral principles for our lives today.

Some of these questions about the content and implications of biblical teaching on ethics produce different answers among different readers. Earlier I talked about the value of assurance, which arises from an evident consensus. The greater the number of significant sources that we can find to support a particular view, the more confident we will be that the view is a responsible one to hold. We know that we need to make a case for the approach that we will take, or that we need to be familiar with the case made by an author whose approach we wish to adopt. We need to be equally clear about our rationale for holding the views that we wish to commend to others, remembering that we respond to these questions within a long tradition of doctrine and prayer. Here we have another example of what I would call a "that/what" distinction. That we recognize the way in which the New Testament presents Jesus as teacher, moral example, and mediator on our behalf is vital for our study of ethics. What precisely he has to teach us in terms of ethics, or what we can and should learn from his moral example, are subjects of further study requiring time, effort, and prayer. In the process we need to build a case for the resulting conclusions that we wish to hold and commend to others.

Before moving to the second way that Christian ethics is distinctive, it may be helpful to take note of three general ideas about how the Bible might be used for ethics. First of all, scripture holds up a mirror to our true human condition. Reading its texts and incorporating their message, we are helped to discern the truth of Paul's unqualified statement that "all have sinned and fall short of the glory of God" (Romans 3:23). Second, the teaching of the Bible can serve as a kind of restraint to our conduct, much in the way that a bookend can help keep upright an unruly shelf of books. Third, the teaching of the Book of Scripture can serve as a map to guide us toward our destination, teaching us the best route to follow.[6] Taking note of these three ideas can help keep us from viewing in too narrow a way the potential significance of the Bible for ethics.

∿ Being in Christ in the Church

We have already seen that discerning ethical principles from our reading of the Bible, even from the recorded teachings of Jesus, does not always lead to full and harmonious agreement. Here is a paradox: the usual condition of our moral awareness that finds reading scripture to be challenging, even problematic, also makes reading scripture and participating in the life of the Christian community necessary. Looking at some familiar prayers can help us to see why this is so. "Holy and gracious Father," we pray in Eucharistic Prayer A, "in your infinite love you made us for yourself" (BCP 362). Yet, to paraphrase Augustine, without God we cannot find God, because our hearts and minds are darkened and our vision is clouded by the fall. Even though God's goodness and love have been made known to us in creation, we become aware that this is not enough. There is a reason why God has also been made known in the Word spoken through the prophets, "and above all in the Word made flesh, Jesus" (BCP 368). As our Eucharistic Prayer B also reminds us, God's Word became incarnate for us in view of our specific needs.

> In him, you have delivered us from evil, and made us worthy to stand before you. In him, you have brought us out of error into truth, out of sin into righteousness, out of death into life. (BCP 368)

Though it is often joked that the fall is the one empirically verifiable doctrine of our faith, we are as apt to ignore it as we are to claim it. Recognize it or not, we are fallen beings, a fact that colors our study of Christian spirituality and moral theology. The teachings and example of Jesus at first seem plainly accessible to us on the written page of scripture; in time, however, we find that we need "the mind of Christ" to enable us to know and follow them because we are still unsure how to live and love, and how to choose God "day by day" in our actions. Some Protestant approaches to Christianity present the Bible as the primary answer to this uncertainty, as if the Bible by itself was the source of Christian life and experience. Anglicans have placed an additional emphasis upon divine grace working through the worshiping community in preparing and forming us to discern within scripture the wisdom that leads to faithful seeing, loving, and following.

We encounter the living Word both in the worshiping community and in scripture. We pray that the same Word of God made present in the eucharist, who earlier inspired the human authors of the Bible, will also inspire us in our reading and learning from scripture.[7] Being in Christ, in his body the church, we are not simply followers of a religion or adherents to a system of beliefs. We participate in the trinitarian life of the *living* God, having been drawn into the inner life of God through baptism. We have been made a new people, who can pray, in the words of the Morning Prayer collect, "Heavenly Father, in you we live and move and have our being" (BCP 100). We refer to this reality quite often in our worship. One of the closing sentences of scripture for Morning and Evening Prayer is taken from the third chapter of Ephesians:

> Glory to God whose power, working in us, can do infinitely more than we can ask or imagine: Glory to him from generation to generation in the Church, and in Christ Jesus for ever and ever. (BCP 102, 126)

The passage directs us toward the power and presence of God working in us as we pursue ethics in daily living, a power that is beyond our imagination and yet active within our earthly humanity. For this reason, the words of the hymn "St. Patrick's Breastplate" are just as appropriate for services of baptism as they are for ordinations. Every baptized person can say,

Christ be with me, Christ within me,
Christ behind me, Christ before me,
Christ beside me, Christ to win me,
Christ to comfort and restore me,
Christ beneath me, Christ above me,
Christ in quiet, Christ in danger,
Christ in hearts of all that love me,
Christ in mouth of friend and stranger.[8]

One of the brief scripture readings provided for
Compline encourages us to be strong in our reliance
on this same truth:

May the God of peace, who brought again from
the dead our Lord Jesus, the great shepherd of
the sheep, by the blood of the eternal covenant,
equip you with everything good that you may
do his will, working in you that which is pleas-
ing in his sight, through Jesus Christ; to whom
be glory for ever and ever. (BCP 132)

In baptism, we are called to live no longer by or for
ourselves, but to God and with God. As Paul proclaims, "I have been crucified with Christ; and it is no
longer I who live, but it is Christ who lives in me"
(Galatians 2:19-20). Although we can overemphasize
our own need to exert initiative as well as the importance of what God alone makes possible, a proper
appreciation for the incarnation calls for a balance
between the two. The fact that Jesus was both fully
human and fully divine reminds us that the plan of
salvation requires both sources of strength in the
Christian life. Our human endowments—assisted,
renewed, and transformed by saving grace—are key
ingredients of the moral life. In Jesus, God is at work
both in us and *with* us.

Writing in the eighth chapter of Romans about our new life after baptism, Paul makes a number of remarkable statements.

> If the Spirit of him who raised Jesus from the dead dwells within you, then the God who raised Christ Jesus from the dead will also give new life to your mortal bodies through his indwelling Spirit. (8:11 NEB)

The translations of *The New English Bible* and *The Revised English Bible* capture this insight about cooperation between human and divine: the "Spirit comes to the aid of our weakness," (8:26) and "in everything, as we know, he co-operates for good with those who love God and are called according to his purpose" (8:28). When we respond in love to God's purposes in redemption for the creation, we find that our efforts to live as God would have us live are enabled and strengthened by the indwelling presence of Christ in the Spirit. Paul's stirring words at the conclusion of the same chapter from Romans have become familiar to many of us because they are often selected for reading at the rite of Christian burial: nothing can separate us from the love of Christ, and from the love of God for us in Christ. In this portion of Romans, we see together the three emphases that distinguish Christian life and Christian ethics: they are God-enabled, Christ-indwelled, and Spirit-led.

With regard to the leading of the Spirit, we can return once again to the collect for mission from the rite for Morning Prayer, which is also a collect for ministry and a prayer for all Christians in their vocation:

> Almighty and everlasting God, by whose Spirit the whole body of your faithful people is gov-

erned and sanctified: Receive our supplications
and prayers which we offer before you for all
members of your holy Church, that in their
vocation and ministry they may truly and
devoutly serve you; through our Lord and
Savior Jesus Christ. (BCP 100)

The whole body of the church is governed and sanctified by the Spirit. In light of this, we pray through the
Lord Jesus that all Christians may truly and devoutly
serve God as an extension of the Spirit's ongoing work
of governing and sanctifying. Here we are developing
the insight we first noted in chapter one. On the one
hand, the righteousness that stems from the Spirit's
governing is present in the true service that we offer.
On the other hand, the holiness that stems from the
Spirit's work of sanctification is present in the devout
service. We can see the same connection that we have
discerned between holiness and righteousness as features of the Christian life after baptism in a prayer
"For all Baptized Christians." Christian ethics are distinctive because we link the character of our new life
after baptism with turning away from sin and with
the indwelling of Christ, "so we may be renewed in the
spirit of our minds, and live in righteousness and true
holiness; through Jesus Christ our Lord" (BCP 253).
Not only do we pray through Jesus to the Father that
our life may be different; we pray that we will also
live in righteousness and true holiness *through him.*

The weekly gathering of the baptized community
in the parish eucharist on the Lord's day epitomizes
all these themes, but habit and attitude sometimes
obscure the radical nature of this God-oriented and
other-oriented act. Eucharistic Prayer C articulates the
challenges we face as we approach the altar.

Open our eyes to see your hand at work in the
world about us. Deliver us from the presump-
tion of coming to this Table for solace only, and
not for strength; for pardon only, and not for
renewal. Let the grace of this Holy Communion
make us one body, one spirit in Christ, that we
may worthily serve the world in his name. (BCP
372)

Christian ethics fundamentally differs from any other
kind of ethics in that it is centered on the continuing
presence of the Lord's self-offering and his offering of
the whole creation to the Father through the Spirit.
Living in the reality of the Holy Trinity makes a difference in the way that we approach each day and its
activities. Our eucharist is a communion with the
Lord and with each other in his one body. It is a communion offered not simply for our restoration from
sin, misfortune, or illness, but also in preparation for
service. "Send us now into the world in peace," we
pray as we close our worship, "and grant us strength
and courage to love and serve you with gladness and
singleness of heart." Another prayer asks, "Father,
send us out to do the work you have given us to do,
to love and serve you as faithful witnesses of Christ
our Lord" (BCP 365-66). As we go forward strengthened by grace through the baptismal and eucharistic
indwelling of Christ, we are witnesses to his teaching,
his pattern of life, and his work of redemption on our
behalf. Truly, Jesus makes a difference in our ethics.

Between the old life and the new, between the
ethics of the non-Christian and those of the Christian,
we can expect to find both continuity and discontinuity. Christians and non-Christians live and work side
by side in the same world, and they perform many of
the same actions. Just as non-Christians are capable

of doing moral good, Christians are capable of moral evil. The Book of Scripture as a source of moral principles and learning does not therefore set Christians utterly apart from others—but it does set them apart. This is one of the most important ways in which moral theology recognizes the value of "both/and" thinking, as contrasted with "either/or" thinking. Christian ethics articulates both the moral good that we share with others and the good that has been specially revealed through scripture, Christian worship, and doctrine, which set the Christian moral life apart from even the highest ethical principles of other religious traditions. The central aspect of this difference is the reality of Christian life after baptism. So what sets Christians apart is not some special knowledge that they alone possess, or a special ability to avoid sin and error in daily life. What sets the pattern of Christian moral life apart is that it is God-enabled, Christ-indwelled, and Spirit-led.

～ Axioms for Moral Theology

10. Anglicans distinguish between moral knowledge, which is revealed to everyone through the Book of Nature, and saving knowledge, which is mediated through the "special revelation" of the Book of Scripture. Saving knowledge shapes life after baptism in such a way as to leave both continuity and discontinuity between the moral knowledge possessed by Christians and that of other people and traditions.

~ Chapter Five

Laws, Manners, and Moral Principles

O Lord, mercifully receive the prayers of your peo-
ple who call upon you, and grant that they may
know and understand what things they ought to
do, and also may have grace and power faithfully
to accomplish them; through Jesus Christ our Lord,
who lives and reigns with you and the Holy Spirit,
one God, now and for ever. (BCP 231)

A man dressed in the coveralls of a hospital maintenance employee stands in the main corridor of the
emergency room, while a young boy lies on a gurney
nearby, groaning in pain. Absorbed with the boy's
condition, the man observes a doctor checking the boy
with a stethoscope and whispers to himself, "Check
the x-ray, check the x-ray!" Suddenly, another doctor,
who is directing the traffic of incoming patients, asks
the man to wheel the boy to an observation room. As
the man in coveralls wheels the boy down the hall-
way, he is observed holding the boy's x-ray up to the
light. After quickly guiding the gurney into an eleva-
tor, the man opens the boy's medical chart, makes
some notations, and signs a consent form for surgery.
The boy is safely delivered to the operating room.

Many of us will recognize this scene from the film *The Fugitive*, which portrays the desperate search by a wrongly convicted physician for his wife's real killer. The scene presents an interesting conflict between several different senses of right and wrong. Because of his status as a convicted murderer, and as a prison escapee, the formerly respected surgeon has no legal right to practice medicine. In spite of this, he makes a medical decision concerning the boy's case and writes orders leading to surgery for the sick child. The man is not the boy's parent, yet he signs a consent form on behalf of the absent mother or father. Further, though the man may formerly have had the privilege of practicing medicine in this particular hospital, he acts without consulting the physicians who have actual responsibility for the boy's care. However, as a result of his quick diagnosis and response, the convicted murderer on the run saves the boy's life.

This incident presents what appears to be a conflict between three different ways of determining what we can or should do. The most obvious standard by which we determine right conduct often seems to be what the law allows or requires, yet at the same time many of us are equally attuned to what social expectations and etiquette ask of us. The question of what is morally right and good is equally demanding: in many situations we experience a conflict between the external requirements of civil law and an internally perceived moral principle. A compact way of identifying these three approaches to determining appropriate behavior is to refer to them as laws, manners, and moral principles. The first thing we should notice is that they often overlap. This can pose a challenge for ethical reflection. If we have not sufficiently clarified the distinctions among them, we can fall prey to a reductionism that assumes in many cases they are the same. For example, what is legally required is quite often confused with what is morally right, while what is morally required can seem little more than what is socially correct.

When placed side by side with laws and moral principles, manners may appear to be a trivial and poor relation. Yet we should be honest with ourselves: manners often provide a common framework for a well-functioning community. Further, social misunderstandings having to do with manners can cause most of us to experience just as much thoughtful reflection, tension, or unease as moral predicaments can. At the same time, social expectations expressed and understood in codes of manners can steer us away from the kind of reflective moral thinking that should shape our ethics. Plays and novels in the style of comedies of manners delight us for this reason; they illustrate with humor how we can be preoccupied with conformity to social standards without really thinking about the true moral good.

The fugitive doctor's situation in the hospital emergency room provides a useful example by which we can recognize some of these distinctions. Inevitably, he faces a personal challenge when he wrestles with whether to act on the boy's behalf. His intervention in the case might easily betray the fact that he is only masquerading as a maintenance employee; saving the boy's life might put him right back on death row. He is surely aware that as a convicted felon, his license to practice medicine has been withdrawn and his civil and legal rights have been significantly curtailed. Yet the call of a higher moral law overpowers any fears he might have about breaking the civil laws of his community and the state's medical licensing regulations. The result is that he engages in an action that may be morally required and right in these circumstances but is legally impermissible. At the same time, social expectations about proper manners closely parallel the legal and moral ones. We are usually expected to consult with others before we do things that involve them, their work duties, or their family members. Though the fugitive doctor fails to observe this common courtesy of social convention, it is a convention that is usually set aside quickly in an emergency.

It is not only dramatic situations like these that can teach something about the similarities and differences among laws, manners, and moral principles. The columnist Judith Martin, better known as Miss Manners, uses gentle humor and a keen eye to explore aspects of our social interaction with others. One helpful bit of insight she offers has to do with being imposed upon. As many of us know, people can abuse our time and attention when they act in a way that depends upon our responding with politeness. Some people specifically take advantage of the fact that children are usually taught not to be rude to nice-talking adults. We can feel unsure about how to respond when those who wish to exploit an open ear corner us. Miss Manners, however, observes that "politeness does not require one to enter into debatable excuses for not doing what one was not obligated to do in the first place. The proper feeling afterward is relief, not guilt."[1] Yet contrary to the refreshing assertions of Miss Manners, we can find ourselves unsettled about the ambiguity between social obligation and moral obligation. At those times when we want to be quiet or to read, we often feel guilty for not responding in friendly conversation when spoken to by someone sitting next to us.

Or consider a case presented with obvious delight by *The New York Times* editorial page called "Michigan's

Cusser Delux."[2] After having difficulty with his canoe a young man was overheard swearing in a loud voice by families in nearby boats. Acting in the interest of the other boaters as well as perhaps the upturned canoeist, a sheriff's deputy issued the young man with a ticket enforcing an 1897 statute prohibiting cursing in the presence of women and children. The _Times_ suggested that "the Michigan judge should dismiss the case quickly," saying that the accused man did not belong in court. Though the editorial was careful to note some examples of communities and citizens who feel strongly about "dirty talking," the newspaper appeared to argue that both the law and the social conventions upon which it is based have passed their time of relevance and usefulness. Whether or not this is so, we still might want to object to the public use of such language on the ground of moral principles.

⟿ The Will of God and the Will of Human Communities

What, if any, is the difference between needing to apologize to another person about a social lapse and needing to apologize to God? In other words, are ethics simply manners writ large? What is the role of society in determining what is right and wrong? These are the kinds of questions we can find ourselves pondering in awkward or unsettling social occasions. We might begin by considering some sentences in the prayer book that speak of sin, as in this form of confession:

> We have erred and strayed from thy ways
>   like lost sheep,
> we have followed too much the devices and
>   desires of our own hearts,

we have offended against thy holy laws,
we have left undone those things which we
        ought to have done,
and we have done those things which we
        ought not to have done. (BCP 62-3)

Here the reference point is the will of God. We confess that we have departed from God's ways and God's holy laws. In prayerfully reciting these words of the confession, we are saying two things. We are acknowledging that we share with others a common condition of willful separation from God that is displayed in our lives and relationships. We are also confessing that we have actively departed from God's will for us through our own choices and acts. If we prepare ourselves ahead of time for this part of the service, some questions may occur to us. Does our failure to conform to civil statutes and laws, or to social norms and expectations, overlap with our "erring and straying" from God's ways? To whom are we accountable when we act contrary to these laws, norms, or divinely given principles? This turns out to be a question with far-reaching significance.

You may remember a story in the church press about a resolution presented a few years ago to the annual convention of the Diocese of Michigan. The convention was asked to endorse this statement: "Jesus Christ is the only name under heaven by which we must be saved." The diocese received national attention when the resolution was defeated and we can easily see why. People could then say, "The Diocese of Michigan has refused to agree that Jesus Christ is the only name by which we must be saved." Among the reasons cited for the defeat of the resolution was the concern that its passage would offend Jews and make Christian–Jewish dialogue more difficult, but I

suspect that there was also some unease about passing a resolution that could later be used as a religious
test against fellow church members who seem overly
flexible in their theology.

This unease is well-founded, though we need to
explore why. In an era when our communities are so
often divided by debates over moral issues, it is common to hear, "It's time someone took a stand!" But
what does it mean to "take a stand"? While I agree
with the statement put forward in the Michigan resolution, I believe I would have voted against it. Why?
Because the way the resolution was worded creates a
confusion between different sources of authority. If
passed, the resolution could have had significant consequences for moral theology had its backers gone on
to propose similar resolutions concerning ethics. Just
imagine a proposed resolution like this one from
Matthew 5:22: "If you say, 'You fool,' you will be
liable to the hell of fire." Taken out of context such
statements may have different meaning. Suppose the
Michigan resolution had been worded slightly differently to read, "_Scripture says_ that Jesus Christ is the
only name . . . . " I could have voted for such a resolution because its source of authority is clearly identified. Even someone who disagreed with the theological
statement at the heart of it could still agree that the
statement is indeed found in the New Testament, and
is proclaimed there on apostolic authority. For the resolution to have been passed without the words
"Scripture says," however, would have made the truth
of the statement depend on the convention's authority and not that of the Bible. It would invite debate
about whether or not it was theologically correct, and
help nurture the idea that diocesan conventions have
the authority to determine church doctrine.

Perhaps you have encountered resolutions presented at your own diocesan convention addressing such
moral issues as sexual relations outside of marriage,
assisted suicide, or state policies concerning the regulation of firearms. Do our diocesan conventions, or
General Convention, create the moral theology of the
church when they pass resolutions and canons? The
question is important. When we put forward resolutions like these we foster the idea that legislative
assemblies have this role. In chapter two we discussed
the three main ways that we can identify the source
of the moral good. We suggested three words as a
helpful way to remember the three concepts: nature,
history, and convention; or, found, received, and
made. Moral principles are found in creation, received
from tradition, or made by choice. To try to remove
moral ambiguity in church affairs by passing resolutions and canons is to encourage the belief that moral
principles are largely an artifact, made by choice and
arrived at through agreement.

One unfortunate by-product of this tendency per-
tains to the question of accountability. If we say that
ecclesiastical legislative assemblies determine the
moral good for the church, we may come to see these
assemblies as the source of authority for the principles. Persons who then fail to live up to the principles
and the regulations based on them may arrive at the
false conclusion that they are primarily accountable
to the institutional church and not to the God in
whose name such institutions purport to act. If it is to
function as an organized community, the church will
necessarily have administrative procedures and regulations that help order its common life and reflect its
central beliefs and moral principles. Nevertheless, a
problem is created when the procedures and regulations are confused with the beliefs and principles they

are meant to express. This insight lies at the heart of
an historic Anglican concern about some aspects of
Roman Catholic ways of viewing the church.

We can put the point this way. The church in this
world may witness best to its moral principles when
it points to the gospel under which Christians and
non-believers both stand. The church and all its members is a hearer of the gospel, standing under its judgment and benefiting from its consoling grace. This is
very different from saying that the church embodies
the gospel so closely that accountability to the gospel
is confused with accountability to the church.
Anglicans believe that the church in this world is a
hospital for the sick, a community of sinners who
share with one another the message of redemption.
This message inspires us to live all the more for God,
in God's ways and for God's ways, as a reflection of
our thanks for the redemption that has been freely
extended to us.

National and diocesan legislative assemblies that
attempt to bring moral clarity to the mind of the
church through the passage of resolutions and canons
risk confusing the nature of our moral accountability.
In terms of basic moral principles we are accountable
to God, in the church; we are not accountable to the
church, in God. This is not to say that we are free to
adopt a libertine lifestyle, claiming that being in Christ
has set us free from earthly regulations. It is only to
try and clarify the true source of authority for any
regulations and procedures the church may need as it
seeks to order its common life in this world.

A seminary classmate gave me a good example of
this difference. A group was organized for high-
school-age members of his parish on the topic of God
and sexuality, and the youth participants were invited by the lay leaders to sign a statement pledging

abstinence from sexual relations before marriage. These pledges would then be given to the rector for safekeeping. The rector, however, declined; he was afraid that this would create a false sense of accountability to the parish clergy in the minds of the youth as they struggled with the challenge of growing into adult sexuality. If they wished to make a pledge to God, all well and good. Yet a problem would develop if a personal sense of accountability to the rector and class leaders preoccupied the youth rather than the question of obedience to God in a Christ-centered life.

∾ Describing and Telling

This last point has implications for how we communicate our moral vision. We may want to shape our moral language by describing the kind of moral good that orients our lives rather than by telling others what moral good ought to shape theirs. We can choose a descriptive approach to moral communication that seeks to *commend* the moral good, rather than a prescriptive one that commands the moral good or forbids the moral evil. When we describe the moral good, we invite others to join us in reflecting on its beauty and wisdom; when we tell them how to behave, we create a gulf and invite them to feel a sense of accountability to us. In the process, we shift a double burden to ourselves that we may not be willing or able to bear. Telling someone what to do invites the reply, "But what if I don't? Then what?" Among the many challenges that prescriptive moral language poses, the prospect of being challenged to back up our moral claims with enforcement may be the most difficult. In addition, when we as a community or as individuals adopt the posture of telling others what to do, we invite close scrutiny as to whether or not we ourselves are above criticism.

A wonderful illustration of the distinction between describing and telling is found in the hiking regulations posted at Grand Canyon National Park. Some years ago, in response to an increase of emergencies and deaths caused by the effects of high temperatures and dry conditions, the park authorities told visitors that they must carry a specified amount of water with them at all times on hikes below the rim. Furthermore, visitors were forbidden to hike down into the canyon after a certain point in the morning so that fewer hikers would be exposed to the midday heat on the trails. Despite the posting of notices to this effect and monitoring by park rangers and guides, hikers continued to head down into the canyon in the heat of the day without sufficient water and suffer heat-related injuries, only to be flown out by helicopter or carried out by mule. After a season or two of these policies, the park embarked upon a new approach. This time, instead of prescriptive regulations telling hikers what to do or not do, new signs stating "HEAT KILLS!" in large red block letters were posted around campsites and at each trailhead. To the delight of officials, the new approach describing the dangers and suggesting precautionary measures proved to be much more successful.

The use of prescriptive language does not always imply the need for enforcement and the threat of sanction. Perhaps you enjoyed reading _Life's Little Instruction Book_ some years ago, which originated as a notebook of maxims written by a father for his son, who was about to head into the world on his own. The book contains a collection of helpful bits of advice from the whimsical (#267: "Lie on your back and look at the stars") to what we might call "just plain old common sense" (#268: "Don't leave car keys in the ignition"). One of my own favorites is #134:

"Don't buy cheap tools."[3] The author is not the least bit shy of telling his son what to do and what not to do, yet the effect of this book is to pass along comforting wisdom rather than impose burdens that cause resentment. The author made it clear to his son that he was passing along maxims that summed up wisdom he had gained over the whole of his life, and he was offering them to his son in the hopes that they might prove equally useful and meaningful.

This is a good example of how we can commend our moral principles to others both within and beyond our church. Instead of trying to address difficult moral issues through the avenue of resolutions and canons—which reinforces the image of an institution externally directing the behavior of others—we can hand on the wisdom we ourselves have received and try to live by. We can commend to others the principles that have challenged us to live well and have held our own conduct to account. In this way, the authority resides in the principles of wisdom and in God, rather than being confused with how that wisdom might be transmitted in the church. As we have suggested, this perception has been a principal feature of Anglican concern about aspects of the Roman Catholic tradition, where the codification of moral principles in canon law has at times resulted in a confusion about where the offense truly lies. Is the greater issue my trespass upon a God-given moral principle, or is it my failure to conform to an ecclesiastical regulation that is said to embody that principle? In organized Christian communities there will always be some degree of overlap between the two, but when they are confused these problems are compounded.

∾ Moral Accountability—To Whom?

Let us return to the three main ways of determining right conduct in daily life that we discussed in connection with _The Fugitive_: laws, manners, and morals. Laws help us to know right and wrong in our public and private conduct, manners help us to know what to do in our social relations with others, and moral principles help us to do the good in our public and private lives. A significant degree of overlap can exist between these three modes of guidance, so that what is illegal can also be immoral as well as a violation of good manners. Yet clarifying the distinction between them will help us to preserve the integrity of each. Wise politicians learn that civil and statutory law cannot require everything that is good, nor can it prohibit everything that is evil. Good and evil actions transcend the scope of legal regulation. The practicality of enforcement is often the arbiter of what can be done through this medium of social organization. For example, the law cannot require us to be kind and considerate to others; it cannot prohibit cheating at golf or require us to write thank-you notes! Can the law even require doctors or nurses to provide medical help for someone in need at an accident scene, outside of their usual working hours and environs? Despite the limitations of law, most people will agree that playing fair golf, writing thank-you notes, and using one's skills to help others in distress are good things to do.

For the sake of understanding the role of moral theology, we need to pursue these distinctions a bit further. We can see on a daily basis that laws are socially regulated in terms of their administration and enforcement. Agents of the community—first the police and then district attorneys and the courts—act in response to breaches of the community will. In the

sphere of etiquette and manners, however, we usually regulate ourselves. Fear of social disapproval can
motivate us to observe good manners, but "enforcement" is self-imposed: no legislature would require us
to RSVP invitations to dinner! But what should we say
about questions of enforcing morals? To some extent,
we can say that morals are enforced by the church
and by society, but this view has its limits. Laws seek
to curb moral evil as well as to promote the moral
good. For example, we seek to curb assault by pun-
ishing those who are convicted of it with fines and
prison terms; we also pass statutes that provide education, medical care, and basic food resources according to various criteria of need. Yet in the end moral
principles, whose source is in the God who made the
heavens and the earth and all of human life, are
"enforced" by the same God upon whose authority
they stand. For this reason, rather than enforce, it
might be better for us to say that the church and society embody or administer morals in specific laws and
social policies that it is their province to enact. We can
enforce what we make, whether it is civil law or social
manners, but we do not "make" moral principles. Our
laws and manners are of course stronger and better to
the extent that they embody moral principles with a
divine source that lies beyond our limited minds and
imaginations.

～ Principles and Policies

There is a further important reason why Christians
should want to pay attention to the old saying, "You
can't legislate morality." Let us suppose that
Christians who serve in Congress have a common
desire to attend to the needs of the poor even though
they belong to different political parties. It is obvious
that Democrats and Republicans often have significant

disagreements concerning policy initiatives designed
to address social problems. What is harder to recognize is that persons who disagree with one another
about policy initiatives can actually share common
principles that provide the foundation for those policies. It is possible that both Democratic and
Republican Christians share a commitment to meet
the needs of the poor, even if they have radically different ideas about how best to enact this commitment
in public policy. Why is this? Because commonly held
principles can give rise to widely different policies and
practices. Here is still another reason why we should
not confuse laws, regulations, or policies with the
moral principles they are said to embody. For if we do,
then we will be liable to confuse loyalty to a policy
with the more general and important matter of faith-
fulness to principle. Indeed, it is often fidelity to principle that can cause high-minded people to disobey
policies that they believe insufficiently manifest, or
even violate, the guiding principles for human life.

By making such a distinction between the principles that give rise to policy and the policies that
embody and manifest principles, we will be able to
reason more effectively with one another about our
disagreements. A theology tutor once shared with me
a saying that goes back at least a couple of hundred
years: "People are more often right in what they
affirm than in what they deny."[4] Although we often
grow more animated over what annoys us, we usually have a deeper commitment to the views we want to
uphold and commend—and more insight about them.
We often disagree about policy initiatives, and by
extension about laws, canons, or regulations. But if
we first focus on our commonly held principles, then
we can reason together as to the policies, regulations,
and rules that might best embody the principles we

wish to affirm. If we have disagreements about principle, then this is certainly where our attention and energies ought to be focused first.

At a time when many are resorting to legislation in order to clarify moral teaching in the church, we would do well to distinguish our desire for moral clarity from the related but very different activity of establishing clear policies for organizing our common life. Whether or not we can regulate the moral conduct of bishops, priests, and deacons, whose ministry is under "orders" to the church, we certainly cannot regulate the moral conduct of most of the church's ministers, the baptized laity. Right now the discussion tends to be centered on issues of marriage and human sexuality, but we could just as easily argue about economic policy or about the use of armed force to confront social evil. This is in no way an argument for moral relativism. On the contrary, the church in its teaching can give voice to the clearest and most unwavering commitment to the poor, to innocent human life, or to the sanctity of marriage. While doing so, we can honestly recognize that there will be some diversity in the way these commitments to principle are embodied in public policy, whether in church or in society.

This insight is related to an axiom we have already identified: legislative gatherings do not make the moral theology of the church—even if they are called to express it in policies that seek to regulate outward aspects of its common life. In many respects the moral theology of the church is not *made*, but rather *found* in the moral principles given to us in the Book of Nature and through the Book of Scripture. The trial by the House of Bishops of their colleague Walter Righter, often portrayed in the press as a "heresy trial," was a low point in the common life of the

Episcopal Church. In most trials, such as the O. J. Simpson murder trial, the purpose is to determine whether the defendant is guilty of certain acts—not whether these acts are against the law. The Righter trial, on the other hand, seemed to have been convened for a larger purpose: to resolve whether ordaining those who engage in sexual relations outside of marriage is contrary to the doctrine and discipline of the Episcopal Church. Going to court in order to determine moral teaching is even more problematic than resorting to resolutions or canons. As I suggested before, regulations and policies are simply unavoidable if we are to have an organized community that is institutionally structured. Nevertheless, we should not confuse civil laws or canons with moral principles. Instead, our goal should be to show that moral principles are a gift that will bring life from within, a dependable leaven for action in the way that yeast serves to raise up loaves, rather than an external source of obligation. After all, what is our goal when we return to our Lord and seek amendment of life? In the words of the General Confession, is it only to "walk in your ways"? Or is it also to "delight in your will" (BCP 360)?

∽ Discerning Our Moral Principles

We have been exploring the similarities and differences among laws, manners, and moral principles, and have concluded that these principles should not be confused with either laws or manners. Where can we find some concrete indication of their content? Once again the prayer book provides a helpful starting point in making a clear connection between moral principles, God's will, and the challenge posed by sin.

It is often the case that in converting to Christianity we experience a growing awareness of the negative effect of sin, and of a life turned in upon itself. This awareness of sin prompts us to seek more earnestly the Christ in whom we find our deliverance. Christian mystical writings often speak of a threefold journey of ascent from "purgation," or separation from all that is not of Christ, to "illumination," our growth into his light, to the experience of "union" with him in the blessedness of divine fellowship. The Christian moral life involves the same journey from repentance to conversion to renewal. Texts from the liturgy of Ash Wednesday provide a helpful reference point for the kind of moral self-examination that lies at the heart of repentance. Reflecting on the Litany of Penitence (BCP 267–269) is not like consulting the tax code, where an outline of regulations could function as a checklist. Novelist Graham Greene provides an ironic view of this approach to moral theology in his novel *Monsignor Quixote*, whose lovable hero faithfully carries around with him Heribert Jone's [sic] *Moral Theology*, first published in 1929 and still in print. The manual gives clear and explicit guidance not only with regard to human actions, but also to their smaller facets, so that the Christian reader could have little doubt about the right thing to do in any situation. With delightful humor Greene shows us how this kind of specificity can provide not only a road map for ultra-conscientious fidelity to the rules, but also allows room for ingeniously conceived moral laxity.

If you read books that describe the history of moral theology, particularly those written by Roman Catholics, you are likely to encounter a lament about "the manuals" and what is called "the manualist approach." Prior to Vatican II many Roman Catholic volumes of moral theology, like the one by Heribert Jone, were analytically deductive, creating the impression that all you had to do was follow all the rules. The moral life is simplified to such an extent that the reader has clear guidance for each and every type of occasion and act. It is not only moral theologians who have raised concerns about this approach, for a recent book by attorney Philip Howard talks about "the death of common sense," whereby increasingly precise and specific laws are passed under the illusion that all ambiguity will be removed in the process.[5] While Howard refers to the need to use common sense in applying general laws to specific cases, moral theologians recognize the importance of using conscience in applying generic principles to particular situations. Making laws or moral rules that are increasingly specific will never make them less generic; we will always have to use discernment and judgment about the proper application of the principle in context. We will return to this point in the following chapters in our discussion of conscience and practical reasoning.

A manual like Jone's *Moral Theology* will always hold an appeal for some of us because conforming to it gives us what Luther would have called a false sense of assurance. In other words, because we have followed the rules, we assume that we are right with God. When contrasted with the manualist approach and the growing trend in statutory law, the much more general phrases of the Litany of Penitence may sound like platitudes. Yet they have their power. Let's focus on some of the specific acts, habits, and dispositions detailed in the litany, addressed to God:

> We have not loved you with our whole heart, and mind, and strength. We have not loved our neighbors as ourselves. We have not forgiven others, as we have been forgiven.

We have been deaf to your call to serve, as
Christ served us.

In the litany, we confess to God:

all our past unfaithfulness: the pride,
hypocrisy, and impatience of our lives...

our self-indulgent appetites and ways, and our
exploitation of other people...

our anger at our own frustration, and our
envy of those more fortunate than ourselves...

our intemperate love of worldly goods and
comforts, and our dishonesty in daily life and
work...

our negligence in prayer and worship, and our
failure to commend the faith that is in us.

And we ask the Lord to accept our repentance:

for our blindness to human need and suffering,
and our indifference to injustice and cruelty...

for all our false judgments, for uncharitable
thoughts toward our neighbors, and for our
prejudice and contempt toward those who differ from us...

for our waste and pollution of your creation,
and our lack of concern for those who come
after us. (BCP 267-68)

These statements provide a substantive group of
moral principles. To discern the basic lines of our
church's moral teaching, we can start with the prayer
book instead of with the journals of the General
Convention or the resolutions of Lambeth Conference.
Within the Litany of Penitence we discover not only

what kinds of conduct "grieve the Holy Spirit," but also what conduct brings joy to the heart of God. For example, when we confess our negligence in prayer and worship, we are invited to form a resolve to attend to prayer and worship conscientiously. When we confess that we have been blind to human need and suffering, or indifferent to injustice and cruelty, we can resolve that our life in the future will be characterized by openness to those who suffer and are in need. We can also decide to oppose injustice and cruelty by working toward a more just world. Of course we must remember that to affirm these significant moral principles in agreement with others is one thing; agreeing about how to implement them in policies and regulations for our common life is quite another. Nevertheless, we possess a much more substantive foundation for our moral theology than we usually give ourselves credit for.

In the next chapter we shall pursue some of the implications of these reflections on laws, manners, and moral principles, as we inquire about several important concepts in moral theology. These will include our view of sin and the vices, the nature of moral character and virtue, and the central concept of conscience.

～ Axioms for Moral Theology

11. The church may adopt one of two postures concerning the relationship between the gospel and the world: it may hold the world up to judgment, or it may witness to the gospel under whose judgment it also stands.

12. The church speaks best to moral principles when it speaks about them descriptively rather

than prescriptively. Describing the moral good invites others to discover its beauty; prescribing the moral good may cause others to feel defensive and suspect us of hypocrisy.

13. Commonly held principles may nevertheless give rise to differing implementations in terms of policy and practice. Just because we agree on our principles does not mean we will agree on how we should live them.

Chapter Six

Sin, Character, and Conscience

> *O God, by whom the meek are guided in judgment,*
> *and light rises up in darkness for the godly: Grant*
> *us, in all our doubts and uncertainties, the grace*
> *to ask what you would have us to do, that the*
> *Spirit of wisdom may save us from all false choic-*
> *es, and that in your light we may see light, and in*
> *your straight path may not stumble; through*
> *Jesus Christ our Lord. (BCP 832)*

As I was writing this book, yet another American high school's name became a household word: Columbine. The statistics in this case were particularly troubling. Two boys went on a shooting rampage that left fifteen dead, with plans laid that could have taken the lives of hundreds more. As with each of the prior cases of school shootings, the difficult question of "why?" was asked once again. But with the tragedy at Columbine, the search for a reason seemed subtly to shift from this or that problem *in* our society to the more disturbing possibility of a problem *with* our society.

The fact that a horrific pattern had been repeated, and repeated on such a numbingly large scale, prompted the renewal of a public discussion. My wife and I were reminded of a similar exchange of ideas that occurred in England some years ago. One late afternoon the news reported an event that shook the nation in a remarkable way. A woman in Liverpool had taken her two-year-old son to a shopping mall. While there, they became separated. Two older boys who were ten at the time apparently befriended the young boy and took him to a railway line, where they beat him and left him for dead. In a country where fewer violent events of this kind are reported in the daily news, the story was especially shocking. Once again the same question was being asked, "What kind of society are we that this could happen in our midst?"

～ Act and Character

The question about what kind of society we are is fundamental because it acknowledges a connection between a community and the behavior of those who live in it, between who we are and what we do. The Christian moral tradition speaks of this connection as the relationship that exists between act and character. The kind of person we are shapes the kinds of things we are likely to do; the kinds of things we actually do give shape to the person we are becoming. In other words, acts shape character and character shapes acts. The beauty of the question asked after Columbine is its recognition of the community dimension of act and character. What I do as an individual will often reflect the way that my society has shaped my character. Equally true, though more uncomfortable to recognize, is the fact that what I do will shape the society I live in.

Because of its focus upon practical reason, moral theology approaches the question of character primarily in relation to action. In Christian ethics, character is usually spoken of as a disposition to act in particular ways. The shape of one's character is significant precisely because it is the key predictor of future behavior. As human beings we are, of course, free to act spontaneously and impulsively in unpredictable ways, and we often surprise one another with unexpected choices and acts. Yet when we come to reflect with others about who we are and what we want to do, the things we have done are always significant. This is true in job and college admissions interviews, in marriage preparation, and in preparation for baptism.

A compelling feature of the early Christian community was the way in which candidates for baptism were often asked to leave certain occupations behind because they were inconsistent with life in Christ. Moreover, candidates for baptism generally took up to three years to assume their place among the communicants around the altar. In this pattern we can recognize an insight that has become significant for the Christian moral tradition: individual acts are important because they become part of patterns of living. Acts that are repeated form habits, and habits create dispositions to act in certain ways. In this way acts slowly build character. Patterns of action that are inconsistent with the good things that we seek can be difficult to leave behind, just as patterns of action embodying those good things are hard to build. On one occasion after another we find the choice to do good a challenge when we are trying to break old habits and build new ones. As we often say too casually about a difficult choice, because we are not always aware of the deeper moral significance, "It's character building!"

This central insight about the relationship between act and character encourages us to reflect on the connection between ethics and spirituality in everyday life as well as in theology. If you read classics in Anglican moral theology like Kenneth Kirk's *Some Principles of Moral Theology* or *The Vision of God*, you will notice a strong interest in what is called the interior life. Since it is important to preserve a balance between act and character, ethics and spirituality, we cannot overemphasize either one. If we focus solely on acts in our ethical thinking, we may ignore the way acts shape character and the spiritual life. In the same way, if we say that what is most important in ethics is character and spiritual growth, we may create the impression that individual acts are not all that significant. Throughout history Christians have vacillated between these two emphases in the moral tradition. Again it is a question of "both/and" rather than "either/or." Our moral theology will be stronger to the extent that we think about both act and character, and the dynamic relationship between them.

In this chapter, we will explore some important features of who we are as moral agents. We will reflect further on the role of sin in the moral life and develop an understanding of moral character in relation to what have been called the virtues and the vices. Finally, we will examine different ways of understanding conscience, which is a central feature of moral consciousness.

～ Life East of Eden

A story is told about a little girl who asked her bishop whether he was saved. In reply the bishop said, "I have been saved from the penalty of sin, I am being saved from the power of sin, and one day I shall be saved from the presence of sin."[1] He may have been following St. Paul's lead in talking about salvation, for Paul frequently spoke of salvation as past, present, and future. At any rate the story illustrates the way that salvation and sin have different dimensions. We have already noticed that when speaking about salvation, we can distinguish but never separate justification from sanctification, because what God freely does _for us_ prepares us for what God freely does _in us_ and _with us._ The bishop's comment about being saved from the penalty of sin refers to justification: when God set aside the penalty of sin in Jesus' death, we were also freed from the power of sin and death by his resurrection. Yet we find ourselves still living into the fullness of that truth; even though it has been accomplished once and for all in principle, the result is not fully evident in practice. So we experience daily life as sanctification: the process of being saved from the power of sin in anticipation of our life around the throne of the Lamb when we will no longer encounter the presence of sin. Though our salvation has been secured for us, we still can identify with Paul's encouragement to "work out your own salvation with fear and trembling." For as he says, "it is God who is at work in you, enabling you both to will and to work for his good pleasure" (Philippians 2:12-13).

As we respond to the great things that God has done for us by giving up our lives to walk in holiness and righteousness, we continue to experience the power of sin in our hearts and minds, in our acts, and in the world of persons and events around us. As Christians, how do we negotiate a course through the tangle of thorns and thistles that still characterize life east of Eden?

It may seem that through our exploration of the Litany of Penitence in the previous chapter we had at last come to the heart of what moral theology is all about: identifying sins and helping us avoid them. Though there is certainly a measure of wisdom here, there is also a potential problem if we make this our focus of attention. Historically, the western Catholic tradition has tended to focus upon sin as particular acts of disobedience and negligence, while the Protestant tradition has tended to focus on sinfulness, the general condition of those who are the children of Adam. In recent times, however, the two have moved more closely together. Precisely how each one of us has inherited the general condition of sin lies beyond moral theology, which simply accepts the idea of original sin as a basic given in Christian doctrine. It shapes our approach to moral theology, as does a proper regard for the continuing signs of the goodness of creation and for God's transforming work in redemption. In focusing on the practical, on our daily "practice" or action, and upon the kinds of thinking and reflection that shape human action, moral theology will tend to focus on sins. Yet we should never lose sight of the forest for the trees. We must also pay attention to the root condition that becomes manifest in a variety of dispositions and actions that plague our daily lives.

One disadvantage of focusing on the identification of sins is that it encourages us to think moral theology is structured around laws, so that we see sins as infractions against those laws. Having identified in the previous chapter the danger of confusing moral principles with the policies, rules, or laws that may manifest them, we need to step back and see the larger point. The moral life is not simply a matter of avoiding missteps and trying to limit the tally of notations in the great record-book of life; it is about holiness and a journey of growth into the glory of the living human person exemplified for us in Jesus Christ. At the end of the Sermon on the Mount when Jesus said, "Be perfect, therefore, as your heavenly Father is perfect" (Matthew 5:48), he was talking about the fulfillment of a potential, not simply the avoidance of mistakes. He is telling us, be brought to your proper completion and fulfillment. His words lead us toward a righteousness exceeding that of the Pharisees who, as he showed us, were absorbed with regulations and policies. Instead, Jesus presents us with a moral vision characterized by beatitudes, by growth-producing principles, and by an encouragement in what the Christian and other moral traditions have called virtue.

It is often said that sins are those things that separate us from God. We might want to rephrase that to say that the condition of sin, resulting from the fall, has separated us from God. To a greater or lesser extent, we all share a common disposition to live apart from God's will that pulls against our baptismal commitment to seek and embody God's will. When we sin, we turn away from God's embrace and nurturing guidance, and we try to live as if we were on our own. Respecting our freedom, God lets us make this choice and allows us to experience the consequences of our own folly. Acts of sin are related to the general condition of sinfulness in two ways. They are particular acts that reflect that general condition and they are also particular acts that separate us from living in active cooperation with God's will and grace. To explain the difference that this distinction makes in our own action, some formal terms have been used in the Christian moral tradition. Based on a distinction implied in certain New Testament texts,[2] Christians speak of *mortal* and *venial* sins. The latter are acts of sin that simply represent the general condition of sin, while mortal sins embody a deliberate and knowing consent to live apart from God's evident will. Though there is debate in the moral tradition about the helpfulness of this distinction, we can certainly recognize various factors that can cause us to view some sins as having more gravity. Knowledge, intention, and the consequences of what we do are all factors that complicate our involvement in acts that reflect a life lived apart from the leading of God.

This correlation between the general internal condition of sin and the way it is manifest in individual acts helps us to see finally how the realm of morals differs fundamentally from that of laws and manners. Our interaction with laws and manners in daily life easily creates the impression that all we have to do in order to be good is decide to follow the rules, and then act upon this resolve. Though laws like the tax codes have become exceedingly complex, and though books of etiquette contain a staggering amount of advice, both of them at least in theory can be learned, known, and acted upon. Yet we know that this is not so with morals. Who among us has not felt Paul's lament in his letter to the Romans?

> In my inmost self I delight in the law of God, but I perceive that there is in my bodily members a different law, fighting against the law that my reason approves and making me a prisoner under the law that is in my members, the law of sin. Miserable creature that I am, who is there to rescue me out of this body doomed to death? God alone, through Jesus Christ our Lord! Thanks be to God! (Romans 7:22-25 NEB)

Though we can discern moral principles and know them in our hearts, we find ourselves resisting them, acting apart from them, and seeking to get around them. A habitual disposition to sin remains in us despite the fact that we have died and risen again with Christ into the new life of the Spirit.

Laws and manners do not ignore internal factors that play a part in human action. When considering charges against someone accused of taking another person's life, it is significant to the enforcement of law whether there was premeditation. Intention and attitude are also of interest in the sphere of morals, yet both law and manners are concerned primarily with outward action and public behavior. Internal issues governing human action are much more important to morals, but not all-important: moral theology is interested in both the outward and inner shape of human acts. That is why a simple ethical code can never serve as a satisfactory basis for ethics even though it results from ethical reflection. Persons act in the world, and not simply bodies. Nor do rules by themselves shape actions. Human beings shape actions. We have ideas, hopes, and memories, and we reflect on principles as we consider what we are to do. As we reflect, we face the challenge of honoring those principles in specific acts that we intend will embody and express them. And we know from experience that this is not always, if ever, straightforward.

∾ Acts, Character, and Virtue

From time to time we meet someone who has the annoying habit of constantly trying to excuse prior behavior. The bottom line seems to be, "I want to be seen for who I am, not what I've done!" This tendency to put some distance between our acts and ourselves may be familiar to us. We may want to linger over the credit we receive for accomplishments but are quick to disown our misdeeds. The old maxim comes to mind: Success has many parents but a failure is always an orphan. We need to acknowledge that everything we do, not just the acts we choose to own, is in some way or another connected with who we are.

Having spoken of original sin as the disposition to live and act in ways that depart from God's will and presence, we can see why the Christian moral tradition is so interested in character. Ethics is interested not only in the quality of our acts, but also in their source. Yes, the fall has had an effect on each one of us, but we still bear the image of God within, even though we have lost likeness with God. It should not surprise us to find that our acts reflect a mixture of intuitive influences, sometimes for good and sometimes for ill, both complementing and competing with our prayerfully reasoned intentions. Modern psychology continues to provide insight about how heredity and social environment can shape the way that we respond to life experiences. Nevertheless, there is a clear role for the exercise of moral reflection: we can form intentions, arrive at a decision, and act. Each one of us takes some responsibility for shaping who we are and who we are becoming by what we intend and how we act. Since what I do will both express something of who I am, and will also shape who I am becoming, my responsibility for my action is significant.

This is the positive reason why the Christian tradition is attentive to the moral significance of individual acts. Of course it is possible to become obsessed with the moral value of individual acts, particularly if we have a tendency to be overly scrupulous as we prepare to offer our sins up to God in confession. We can also become careless about the moral significance of what we do, neglecting to consider how our acts may grieve both our neighbors and our Lord. Yet each act of ours is potentially very significant. As we have noticed, acts are repeated, and repeated acts form habits. What may have begun with careful reflection soon becomes unconscious; habits become dispositions to act and respond in consistent ways, whether for good or for evil. Acts are the building blocks of habits, and habits are the material for the dispositions that constitute our moral character.

Human beings respond to life experiences with a real mixture of dispositions. Just as there are physiological characteristics that we share with each other, there are also certain psychological characteristics pertinent to moral action that we share as well. These are the virtues and vices that feature in the moral vocabulary not just of Christians, but of the non-religious world as well. Virtues are capacities or strengths of character that are exercised and developed in good moral action. Plato, Aristotle, and Cicero all spoke of four "cardinal virtues"—cardinal from the Latin root meaning "hinge." Many kinds of action that embody the good turn, or hinge, on the four cardinal virtues of prudence, justice, temperance, and fortitude (or courage). Sometimes they are also called the natural moral virtues because they are not dependent upon the special revelation of scripture, but can be found among all persons and societies. Among them, prudence plays a particularly important role in moral theology, for it is the virtue of practical reasoning—reasoning toward action or practice. Our moral tradition has long recognized that a basic, God-given disposition toward the good is common to most people even if it has become corrupt and egocentric. This basic disposition toward the good reveals itself consistently in human character, so that prudence, justice, temperance, and fortitude are four principal ways that the inclination to seek and exemplify the good is manifest in human character and action.

The Christian moral tradition has broadened the concept of the virtues by the addition of the three so-called theological virtues of Paul's first letter to the Corinthians: faith, hope, and love. As gifts of grace, they are called theological virtues to distinguish them from the natural moral virtues given to us in creation. The natural moral virtues stand in the same relationship to the theological virtues as the Book of Nature does to the Book of Scripture. In both cases the former is graced by special revelation that opens and transforms the natural toward its fulfillment within God's plan of redemption.[3] Through the grace of the Holy Spirit, Christ works within us, leading us beyond our natural end to the true good in him. The virtues become more than avenues for our choice to act in certain good ways; they are transformed into channels for the Spirit's leading in the moral life.

Our common disposition to act sinfully is manifested in equally consistent ways, through a pattern of vices we call the seven deadly sins. These seven vices reveal the ways that our basic disposition toward sin is shown in our character and our actions. Pride often comes first because in many ways it is the springboard of the rest, and therefore the most dangerous. Pride is thinking and acting as if we can be free of God's will and flourish on our own. There is a simple memory device that can help us to remember the seven deadly sins: sin *plagues* us. Plagues: Pride, Lust, Avarice, Gluttony, Wrath ("u" stands for the double-u: w!), Envy, and Sloth. They are also called the "capital" sins, for each is the head, or source, of a number of related sins. Calling them the seven deadly sins, therefore, can obscure an important point, for each vice points not toward one particular type of action, but rather to a whole pattern of related actions. In his fine book on the subject, William Stafford suggests that we think of them as "seven terminal spiritual illnesses" that "may give rise to specific actions of a thousand different kinds."[4]

One of the forms of the General Confession we recite in the liturgy refers to "what we have done" and "what we have left undone" (BCP 360). These are the sins of commission and omission, and they refer to wrong acts committed and good acts that we did not pursue. This is the difference between one employee who shares malicious and unsubstantiated gossip about some fellow workers, and another who says nothing and even laughs nervously when a series of inappropriate jokes are told at the expense of those same workers. Another equally important distinction concerns the difference between an active or passive consent to the disposition to sin. For example, when we are passive in the face of sin's influence, we have simply failed to stop the disposition from becoming manifest in particular acts. At other times, we actively consent to the disposition and we act in recognizable ways that manifest the tendency toward sin. Imagine someone who has a tendency to spend inordinate amounts of money on compact disks at the expense of his responsibilites, and who simply gives way to the impulse every time he passes a music store. This passive consent becomes active when the person begins to make calculated plans for how he can make similar purchases by delaying the payments, or borrowing money he cannot repay.

There are a number of important matters that connect with this theme of character. Here we are at the point of intersection between moral theology and ascetical theology, or the study of spirituality. Though the two have often been treated together in the Anglican moral tradition because both are concerned with our growth into Christ-likeness, there are good reasons to look at them separately. Moral theology focuses on the sphere of action and pays proper attention to the realm of praxis, our involvement in concrete acts and our reasoning about them. By contrast, ascetical theology has a special interest in those aspects of our interior life that enhance or hinder our ability and inclination to act upon moral principles.[5]

~ Maps of the Soul

On a wall in the Spanish Chapel at the church of Santa Maria Novella in Florence you will find a fresco painting depicting black and white dogs chasing brown wolves. Our art historian-guide suggested to our group that the painting depicted something of the occasional flares of tension that erupted in the medieval period between the Dominicans and other orders and groups, principally the Franciscans. As we considered the painting, we were invited to look at a map of Florence. Santa Maria Novella, the Dominican church, is built diagonally across the city center from Santa Croce, the Franciscan church. Apparently such a placement was neither accidental nor unusual. In the fresco at Santa Maria Novella, one can easily see that the black and white dogs serve as a not-so-subtle metaphor. They stand guard at the Pope's feet guarding sheep, and they chase brown wolves who threaten the Lord's flock. The Dominicans who wear black and white are portrayed as the Hounds of the Lord, based on a play on Latin words: *Domini Canes* (Dominicans).

Dominican theology tended to highlight the role of reason, both in the way that it viewed the moral life and in the way that God was seen as the author of a rational moral good. Franciscans, by contrast, tended to emphasize the exercise of the will and the movement of the affections, or feelings, in their approach to the moral good and the spiritual life. It is interesting to see how this second approach, which was strongly influenced by the thought of Augustine, went on to influence some Protestant Reformation understandings of the human person and morality. The Catholic tradition, without abandoning the thought of Augustine and later Franciscan theologians, came to place particular emphasis on the approach of Thomas Aquinas and the role of reason.

This tendency to favor some aspects of human moral subjectivity over others is something to which all Christians seem prone. We tend to choose either a reasoned approach to ethical principles or an approach that emphasizes the will and the affections. In this way our view of the human person and how we see the relationship between different aspects of consciousness play a significant role in our ethics. Are reason and the affections naturally competitive in struggling for influence over our wills? Are physical and sensual feelings morally subordinate to thinking? Stretching the metaphor from the fresco in Florence, would we depict the moral life as a struggle between the hounds of reason who protect the lamb of the soul from the wolves of the emotions and feelings? If these questions seem a little abstract, consider for a moment how answers we give to them may shape our sexual ethics or our approach to end-of-life issues. For example, if our concept of what it is truly human is bound up too closely with a narrow view of reason, then the realm of feelings and the body may appear less than human. And what if we happen to experience a conflict within ourselves between feeling and thinking?

We might want to ask, is this how God really created us? These questions can help us to reflect on the ways that we think about our experience. For example, we tend to associate thinking with the head, feelings with the torso and the "heart," and sexual passion with the genitals. Yet it may well be that people in other cultures think differently about the structure of their conscious experience. We also tend to divide up our consciousness into separate faculties, such as reason, will, emotions, and physical sensations. If asked to draw a "map of the soul" many of us will draw a large circle with a number of smaller circles within it, each depicting one of these facets of consciousness. If we make such a drawing, what do the lines represent? A number of contemporary writers are challenging these models by asking us to consider how the use of reason is colored by feeling, and how emotions "have reasons." In an effort to recover a more biblical view of human embodiment, many theologians are calling for us to recover a more integrated view not only of the emotions but also of our sexuality.

As we go on to consider various understandings of moral conscience, we will be helped by a more integrated approach—"both/and" rather than "either/or"— especially in considering the relation between thinking and feeling. The choice to act in a particular way results from more than simple rational deduction, and more than intuition or "gut feeling." Perhaps even more than we recognize, thinking and feeling together inform our reflection upon past acts, as well as our process of shaping a resolve to future action. Instead of driving a wedge between the language of "I thought that" and the language of "I felt that," we might try using words that include and express both. We might say, "I reflected that" or "I settled on this choice."

～ The Question of Conscience

In the 1940s, a Christian pastor in Germany faced a difficult decision. Should his Christian principles guide him to take some decisive steps in shaping the future of his nation? Should those steps involve an act of political murder, so that the suffering of untold numbers of persons would end, and peace might come?

Could a follower of the Jesus who said, "Blessed are the peacemakers," join in a plot to murder Adolf Hitler? Such a plot was indeed uncovered and evidence was found linking at least one Christian pastor to the plan. The pastor was, of course, Dietrich Bonhoeffer, who was hanged in a prison camp just days before it was liberated in April, 1945.

We usually call the kind of terribly difficult decision that Bonhoeffer wrestled with a test of conscience. If we read the newspapers and church press today, we will notice how frequently people appeal to conscience and its guiding role in moral decision-making. The dictate of conscience is often given a privileged place when we are called to give an account of why we have made certain ethical decisions. But what is conscience? Is it the voice of God speaking quietly within us? Is it a tool that we use in order to steer ourselves through a crisis? A strong feeling that we should do something? Or the accumulated voices of parents and elders that have come to shape our attitudes to life? Once again, asking some questions can help us gain some insight about an important moral concept. In the remainder of this chapter we shall explore some different concepts of conscience, and in the next we will consider the exercise of conscience.

One familiar view of conscience is found in Walt Disney's *Pinocchio*, where Jiminy Cricket assumes its role. You probably remember the scene: Jiminy Cricket has just settled in for the night in the home of Geppetto, the clock and toy maker. Just before going to sleep a wistful Geppetto wishes on a star. Then, before Jiminy Cricket has fallen asleep, a fairy comes and gives Pinocchio the gift of life. "Am I a real boy?" he asks. The fairy says no, but that it is up to him to make Geppetto's wish come true. If Pinocchio proves himself brave, truthful, and unselfish, someday he will become a real boy. "You must learn to choose between right and wrong," the fairy tells him.

"But how will I do that?" he wonders. She tells him that he must learn to listen to his conscience. "What are conscience?" he asks.

"What are conscience!" Jiminy exclaims. "I'll tell you what a conscience is. A conscience is the still small voice that people won't listen to. That's just the trouble with the world today."

"Are you my conscience?" Pinocchio asks him.

"Who, me?" he asks. And the fairy asks him if he would like to be Pinocchio's conscience. After he bashfully agrees, she officially makes him Pinocchio's conscience, asking him to kneel as in a knighting ceremony.

"I dub you Pinocchio's conscience, lord high keeper of the knowledge of right and wrong, counselor in moments of temptation, and guide along the straight and narrow path." At this moment she touches him with her wand and momentarily transforms his appearance with a glow.[6]

Here we find a classic account of what conscience is. Conscience holds the knowledge of right and wrong, and provides moral guidance in the face of temptation and uncertainty. What is not so obvious, especially when presented in a story like Pinocchio, is the way in which conscience is portrayed as something outside of "us." If conscience, like Jiminy Cricket, is something that speaks to us or is someone who advises us, then how can conscience be "us"? This may just be a manner of speaking, as when someone who has stubbed a toe cries out, "My foot is killing me!" Clearly the speaker does not mean to imply that the foot is different from the one who cries out. But we should be careful, because habits of speech often indicate how we actually think about and respond to the world. And many if not most of us tend to think of conscience as something apart from us that acts upon us, and is separate from our own agency. It is quite natural for us to say, "My conscience is bothering me," but the wording does suggest that "my conscience" is different from "me."

The other thing we should notice about Jiminy is that he is mystically ordained to his role as moral guide. He is touched with the wand and glows for a moment. Conscience is often thought of as the mystical voice of God, speaking from beyond. Therefore, we feel that it should be followed, even when it goes against reason and common sense. Friends and relatives shake their heads when we tell them that we _just have to_ do this or that, because our conscience tells us so. And there is a certain truth here, for conscience has often been spoken of as the voice of God in the Christian soul. Our moral tradition has long recognized a rule about conscience: conscience must always be followed.

What about other images for conscience? Another popular way of thinking about conscience sees it as functioning like a compass which, if it is working, always points to true north.[7] Just so, we might say that our conscience, like an internal moral compass, always points to the true good. Here we speak of conscience as our moral guide, especially when we are in ambiguous circumstances, and we do not know what to think. We are not sure what principles ought to guide us, and we may be confused about how to apply them to our circumstances. So we rely upon an intuitive feeling, and follow its direction. There is a degree of truth here as well. The Christian tradition at its best has recognized that conscience involves the feelings as well as thought and reason. The Christian tradition has also recognized the way that God sometimes speaks to us through dreams and strong feelings.

Some modern critics want us to see conscience in very different terms. Be careful about relying too much on it, they say, especially if it involves feelings. For conscience, we are warned, is simply the accumulated residue of a lifetime of teaching by our parents and elders. What our elders have told us, we now confuse with the truth. Conscience in this view is therefore a lot like what Freud called the superego: it is the result of our social conditioning. Surprisingly, there is also an element of truth here as well. The Christian tradition has always recognized another rule about conscience. In addition to the rule that conscience must be followed, Christians have said that conscience must be educated. As something that can be trained and formed, it involves our own thinking and reason as well as feelings and intuition from beyond us.

Clearly these are different views of conscience and yet there might well be some truth in each one of them. How are we to think of Christian moral conscience as our guide toward good deeds and holy living? How does conscience function to guide us toward our goal of greater fellowship with God, and the communion of saints in heaven? For me, the most helpful way to think about conscience is to think of it as an activity rather than as a thing. Conscience is what we *do* rather than something we use or possess. Instead of a compass that we consult, conscience is better seen as the *activity* of consulting—of looking, thinking, reflecting, and evaluating. Think of the moral life in terms of a sea kayak in which you are paddling along the shoreline. You come to a bay that you have never explored. How will you negotiate a way through it? How will you avoid hidden sandbars, or dangerous currents, or things that could lead you astray? Several things become helpful. First of all, it is useful to have a map. A chart will tell you what others who have been here before have learned from their experience of this place. It is also helpful to notice the buoys and markers as you head into the bay. Even though this body of water is new to you, the buoys that you recognize from other places will help guide you here. And of course, you will want to consult your compass, which will give you a further point of reference.

The Christian moral life, in our journey toward greater union with our Lord, involves many encounters with unknown places. We must frequently decide what to do in new and even confusing circumstances. It is helpful to be familiar with the experience of others who have gone before us, who have wisdom to share with us about those same challenges. It is also helpful to be familiar with the basic principles of Christian faith and ethics. We will want to know the basic questions to ask in new situations, just as we want to use the buoys to guide us in new and unfamiliar waters. And finally, we need a compass. We need a Christian character that has been shaped through practice, and which is open to the voice of the Holy Spirit. Christian conscience involves each and every one of these things as we steer our course through life. We must both think and feel, we must both remember and plan, and we must both hear and act. Involving all of these aspects of ourselves, conscience is the process of bringing the fullness of the Christian vision to bear upon a single choice.

The exercise of conscience is inescapably personal and individual, but never fully private. I depend on the wisdom of the Christian community as I seek to educate my conscience. And even though only I can exercise it, I depend on the Christian community for guidance on how to do this. As I grow into Christian maturity, I recognize that even my private actions have public consequences. I will recognize that my acts will to some extent reflect the character of my community as well as serve to shape it. Therefore my Christian community will, in the end, have a stake in how I exercise my conscience. In the Revelation to John we hear, "See, the home of God is among mortals. He will dwell with them; they will be his peoples, and God himself will be with them" (Revelation 21:3). In Christ, we never act alone, and never for ourselves alone. As part of a body where all are members one of another, and all are called to building up the body, the exercise of conscience will always occur somewhere on a continuum between two poles. My exercise of conscience will express my personal freedom in Christ, but it always functions within the reality of my relationship with our Lord within his body.

∼ Freedom in Christ

We must ask ourselves, from what has Christ come to set us free? Is our freedom not in part a freedom from the law? Asking these questions can help us to notice where Christian ethics may diverge from the prevalent assumptions of our society, and the ethics of other traditions. A common way of defining freedom is to think in terms of the absence of limits: we can pursue what we wish without hindrance. The language of the New Testament seems to give some support to this approach when we find statements about freedom from the law, sin, and death. These are qualified statements, and quite often statements with further qualifications follow. We have not only been set free from this or that. We have been set free for Christ, whom to serve is "perfect freedom" (BCP 99). Christian freedom is paradoxical, for it is freedom discovered in voluntary service. The word used by Jesus to describe us as his "servants" can also be translated as "slave."

Just as we have found it to be true concerning the moral life as a whole, freedom for Christians can best be described in terms of the fulfillment of a potential. We have been set free to flourish in Christ, and we should not be surprised if the path toward our true flourishing involves a pattern and order. As we grow in this freedom, we discover the joy that can be found in the fulfillment of expectations and of responsibility. In connection with this theme, you might ponder the implications of a collect from the prayer book called "A Prayer of Self-Dedication," which centers on making a voluntary commitment to be God's servant. As you read or pray each phrase, think about what kind of freedom the prayer holds up as characteristic of Christian life. Is it the absence of limits, or the fulfillment of potential?

> Almighty and eternal God, so draw our hearts to thee, so guide our minds, so fill our imaginations, so control our wills, that we may be wholly thine, utterly dedicated unto thee; and then use us, we pray thee, as thou wilt, and always to thy glory and the welfare of thy people; through our Lord and Savior Jesus Christ. (BCP 832-33)

∽ Axioms for Moral Theology

> 14. Acts shape character, and character shapes acts. Character is the disposition to act in particular ways. Individual acts are the building blocks of habits, and habits are the material of dispositions to act in particular ways.

15. As a gift of creation, all people share a basic disposition to seek the good, but as a result of the fall we seek to rule ourselves. These basic dispositions give rise to specific dispositions we call the natural moral virtues and the vices that shape moral action.

16. Moral conscience involves the whole person, both thinking and feeling. It also involves the interrelated acts of reflection upon, and deliberation toward, moral action. Conscience must be followed, but conscience must also be educated.

Chapter Seven

Love in Acts, Rules, and Principles

*O God, you have taught us to keep all your com-
mandments by loving you and our neighbor: Grant
us the grace of your Holy Spirit, that we may be
devoted to you with our whole heart, and united to
one another with pure affection; through Jesus
Christ our Lord, who lives and reigns with you and
the Holy Spirit, one God, for ever and ever. (BCP
230-31)*

It shouldn't have surprised me to see that when people went from church to church looking for help in
a rural county seat town, they often collected duplicate vouchers for food and gasoline, just as they did
in Memphis. Naively, however, I had not expected the
same thing from some of the residents of Paris,
Tennessee, a town of about twelve thousand. I had
called Harry Flowers, the pastor of the local
Presbyterian church, and asked him what he thought
of starting a joint food bank and assistance program
in Paris. Inspired by his enthusiastic response, we
picked up almost a ton of donated food from a large
resource pantry in nearby Jackson. Agreeing that we
should follow the words of Jesus and give freely to
those in need, Harry and I put up notices and placed

an ad in our newspaper. When we opened the following Wednesday afternoon, we expected a handful of people. Much to our surprise and embarrassment, a huge crowd arrived and most of the food was gone in less than two hours!

The incident was a reminder to Harry and me that setting conditions does not diminish the principle of loving others and giving freely. The food was intended for those in need, but we suspected that more than a few of those who had carted away full bags of food had simply taken advantage of our generosity. Then a parishioner of mine who worked at an area government office distributing state and federal aid offered to provide screening of those who might benefit from the church's help. The government officials were pleased at the prospect of having another community resource to which referrals could be made; at the same time, they had the means of verifying an applicant's level of need. This would allow us to solicit donations from churches and the community while providing an assurance that donations would be given to those who could most use it.

Love and rules are not opposed to one another. Indeed, love often requires rules so that the truly loving thing can be done. When working with street people in Memphis, for example, I learned that giving cash to those who ask for it can endanger both them and the church volunteers who were identified as providers of money. Furthermore, giving cash to someone who has a chronic substance abuse habit may be far from the loving thing to do. We may be moved by Paul's observation that the one who loves his or her "neighbor has satisfied every claim of the law" (Romans 13:8, NEB), yet we cannot build a whole ethic upon that verse alone. Paul's point is not that simply by loving we have all the ethics we need.

On the contrary, true love in action is love that fulfills everything for which the law asks. In going on to write that "love does no wrong to a neighbor; therefore, love is the fulfilling of the law" (Romans 13:10), Paul is telling us one of love's rules.

Although it has been almost forty years since the Anglican ethicist Joseph Fletcher first published *Situation Ethics*, his approach to ethics is still very popular in our society. Advocates of this approach like to point out that human beings and situations are unique and particular, while rules and principles are abstract and generic. How do we connect rules and principles with unique situations and people without being arbitrary? For this and other reasons, Christian situation ethicists have tended to say that there is only one valid, universal rule to guide us when we have to make decisions about unique situations: pay attention to the particulars of the situation and then do the most loving thing.

Situation ethicists were not the first to notice this gulf between generic principles and particular situations, but they have been the most persuasive in saying that the leap from the generic to the particular is problematic. Yet don't we make this leap every day? For example, very few of us question what is a routine occurrence in most American cities. Every day our courts have proceedings to determine whether an accused person is guilty of a specific, but also a generic, charge. A criminal investigation will often follow when a death has occurred from something other than natural causes. If someone is subsequently apprehended, it makes sense to us that the person is charged with accidental homicide, manslaughter, or murder in the second or first degree. Because the distinction between these charges appears reasonable and appropriate, we do not say that the courts and prosecutors are creating fictions or being arbitrary. In the same way, in the sphere of manners and social customs, we also find it helpful to make generic distinctions between kinds of situations and kinds of actions.

Is ethics any different in this respect? In dealing with ethical decisions, should we say that we do not recognize kinds of actions and kinds of situations as we do with laws and manners, but only an endless sequence of utterly unique situations and actions? When we ask the question this pointedly, we can begin to see that we may have another "both/and" distinction that has been pushed into an "either/or." Persons and situations are both unique and also share common traits and patterns. In our ethics we could choose to place an emphasis upon either one, but why do so?

Asking these questions can help us to identify a number of issues we will want to explore in this chapter. We will look at the role of conscience in discerning generic moral principles and applying them to the particular circumstances of our daily lives. This will lead us to the challenge posed by the apparent gap between the moral principles we wish to affirm and the actual practices of our own community. Finally, we will want to look at the proper role of discernment and judgment in moral reasoning, as well as the question of who or what gives our acts their meaning.

～ The Exercise of Conscience

Let's look at how ethical questions are often asked. Suppose that the members of the church's Mary and Martha Guild have requested a speaker to come and address their next meeting about the issue of carrying handguns. The state has just passed an ordinance permitting citizens to carry concealed weapons, and many of the women are concerned about personal safety in the urban areas of the diocese. What should the speaker say to them? Or suppose that an elementary school-age child in the parish Christian education program asks his teacher a question about fairness and honesty. The day before, when he was at the hardware store buying a new inner tube for his bike, the cashier gave him change for a ten-dollar bill instead of a five. Having stuffed the money into his pocket, the boy did not notice the error until he got home and counted the change. He asks his teacher whether he has to return the difference, given that the mistake was not his. Are we to approach the ethical questions raised in these two examples as if they were the same kind of question?

Though both examples deal with ethical questions, the first is a generic question raised by a study group while the second is a particular question raised by an individual about a particular situation. The differences between them are significant. The parish study group is asking a generic question: What should someone do in this kind of a situation? The boy in Sunday school, however, asks, "What should I do in this situation? Should I return the five dollar bill?" Let's consider why this distinction is important.

When we ask ourselves the "What should I do here and now?" type of question, we engage in an act of conscience. To answer it, we first need to consider what ethical issues are actually involved and which generic moral principles have a bearing on the question being asked. The second step in the act of conscience is making a connection between these generic principles and the particular situation at hand. Let's explore the case of an eighteen-year-old high school graduate who asks herself, "Should I enlist in the army this week?" One moral principle that might help her arises from a story she remembers from the gospels in which a centurion—a Roman soldier—asks Jesus for help in healing his servant. Jesus, after hearing the centurion refer to the obedience of soldiers under his own command, says, "Go; let it be done for you according to your faith" (Matthew 8:5-13). The young woman considering enlistment notes that Jesus does not tell the man to lay aside his sword or abandon his occupation, so faithful obedience to Jesus may not necessarily require us to forego a similar profession. This is just one of a number of principles that she could arrive at through a process of reflection and discernment. Eventually she will need to make a connection between the principles she has identified and the particulars of her own situation. For example, she might ask herself if Jesus' conversation with the centurion really has a direct bearing on her own question. Assuming that Jesus really did mean for the centurion's occupation to pass without comment, she must ask herself a further question. Is the issue of remaining in military service after one comes to faith in Jesus, as was the case with the centurion, the same as the issue of joining the service when one is already Jesus' follower?

The Christian moral tradition understands the exercise of conscience as these two actions: the discernment of generic moral principles and their application to particular circumstances. Though there is no need to remember the technical terms for these activities, *synderesis* and *syneidesis*, it is worth observing that the second concept has also been called *conscientia*. When you notice how this Latin word *conscientia* is a cognate of our English word "conscience," you can see how confusion could arise. Though the exercise of conscience involves both discernment *and* application, the Latin word confusion has led some to restrict it merely to the latter. If the function of conscience is only to apply principles to particular situations, whose role is it to discern these principles? From here, it is only a short step to saying that the discernment of generic moral principles is solely or at least primarily the work of church authorities, whether the House of Bishops or the papacy. The central point is this: Are you and I, as individual baptized members of the church, responsible for discerning moral principles as part of the workings of conscience? If we say yes, this answer does *not* mean we no longer benefit from the guidance provided by the Christian moral tradition and our respective church authorities.

It is part of the strength of the Anglican tradition to recognize that the discernment of generic moral principles is a corporate activity of the church, taught by the Lord and led by the Spirit. That is why we are cautious about accepting acts of moral discernment by individuals and groups as authoritative and binding on the whole community when they are not supported by the tradition and wider fellowship of the church. Remember the two rules of conscience from the previous chapter: I am to follow my conscience but I am also to educate it. The function of conscience is unalterably personal and particular. Other persons can play a role in educating my conscience by influencing my moral reflection, but only *I* can arrive at what I consider the right decision for me to act on, here and now. Although both church and state institutions and officials can influence my acts of conscience, in the end these decisions can only be mine. No one else can make them for me.

This is why it is problematic to ask another person, "What should I do?" It appears to invite someone else to engage in an act of conscience for me. For the request to be handled responsibly, the friend or spiritual guide who is consulted needs to do one of two things. The first is to make clear that she is joining the questioner in an act of imagination: "If I were *you* in this particular situation, this is how I imagine it would look." Such a reply engages the questioner in discernment's task of exploring principles and application's task of weaving them with the particulars at hand. Alternatively, the friend can make clear that she is imagining herself in the same situation: "If I were in this situation, here is how I think it would look to me." In this way, sympathetically and imaginatively, we can join with others in exploring—even wrestling with—moral questions. But we can never engage in an act of conscience for another person.

This friend or spiritual guide could also suggest exploring the ethical question some other way. "Let's look at your question like this," she might say. "Let's ask, 'What should someone do in this kind of a situation?'" Such an approach can often lead to more effective reflection by opening the door to a broader process of discernment rather than limiting it to the situation at hand. In effect, it makes it more likely that brainstorming can occur.

Those engaged in pastoral care or spiritual direction often find themselves in the difficult situation of being asked to respond to questions that involve ethical principles. They are asked to assist with a personal act of conscience while at the same time they are exploring different facets of a moral issue. In a pressing pastoral situation, priority must be given to the perceptions, feelings, disposition, and circumstances of the person seeking an answer. Moral questions, on the other hand, are best explored on a generic plane, which allows time for reflection and deliberation without the need to come to an immediate decision.

This helps us to see why the church, when engaged in the corporate process of discernment over issues of moral theology, is often better served by starting with general reflection on moral principles than with the specifics of particular cases and situations. Otherwise we will be tempted to limit the scope of our discernment to the cases actually at hand. That is why we need to begin by asking, "What *kinds* of situations, actions, and issues do these cases represent? What others are we overlooking? What do these cases teach us about persons in other particular situations?" Such questions stand behind the old maxim, "Hard cases make for bad laws." Too limited a starting point may yield too limited a conclusion.

⟡ The Gap Between Principles and Practice

At this point we need to explore a bit further what it means to say that moral principles are generic. In this book I have usually contrasted the word "generic" with the word "particular." Unlike the difference between two apparently similar words, general and specific, which is only a difference in scale, there is a qualitative difference between the generic and the particular. Something is either generic *or* particular. The key point is that moral principles are always generic, no matter how specific they become. As an example, let's look at a common moral principle that can be stated in two ways: "Always tell the truth" or "Do not lie." For Christians and Jews, this is the commandment that tells us not to bear false witness, or not to lie. This commandment is both generic and general in its scope and range of application. It is not qualified in any way.

Suppose we were to make the rule more specific: "Do not lie to fellow church members." And what if we make it even more specific: "Do not lie to church members during the coffee hour." The commandment is still generic. What if we were to make it ridiculously specific? "Do not lie to fellow church members during the coffee hour, when they are holding a cup of coffee and wearing a red sweater." Curiously enough even though the rule has become highly specific in its scope and range of application, it still remains generic. I must still personally apply the rule to the particular circumstances in which I find myself by asking a series of questions: Am I talking with a fellow church member, and is it during the coffee hour? Is this other person holding a cup of coffee, or is that tea or hot chocolate she is sipping? Is her sweater red, or is it actually carmine or burgundy? In other words, is this the kind of situation that the very specific but still generic rule is meant to govern? Whether or not this process of applying the generic principle to a particular circumstance seems straightforward, when the stakes are high the presence of any degree of ambiguity can cause us a great deal of difficulty. We are all familiar with the kind of self-doubt that can creep into our reckoning.

Most of us have heard of the formal term for this second activity of conscience, which applies generic principles to particular circumstances. It is called *casuistry*, a word that now has negative connotations. Why? Perhaps it is because we live in an age and a society that is more permissive about moral conduct and tends to emphasize flexibility in the application of principles to circumstances. It is also an age of greater sensitivity to the uniqueness of persons and situations, with a greater skepticism about universals. But despite its negative associations, casuistry can be practiced in a wide variety of ways. It can seek to honor a moral principle to the fullest extent possible; people who take this approach believe that rules should be applied with great rigor even if we have significant doubts about them—hence the term *rigorist*.

By contrast, casuistry can also be practiced in a way that maximizes our freedom of choice by emphasizing the gap between generic principles and particular circumstances, and by highlighting any doubts we may have about the applicability of rules to those circumstances. People who pursue this approach seem lax in their application of rules—hence the term *laxist.*

Many writers and thinkers in the history of moral theology have made a case for steering a middle course between these two approaches. They have rejected a simple choice between rigorously following rules regardless of circumstantial considerations, and setting aside rules in favor of those circumstantial factors. These thinkers recognize that we are rarely dealing with certainties when it comes to making a connection between generic principles and particular circumstances. Nevertheless, when the connection between rules and situations does not seem clear, we should focus our attention on what is probable.

Then the question is one of deciding how much assurance we need. Some theologians argue that, in situations where we are not sure about the application of a moral principle, we should choose the path that is more probable because we have greater assurance for it. We would find out which view had the greatest number of sound arguments, supporting biblical texts, and the consensus of reputable authorities on its side. Other theologians think that in such situations where we are not sure about the application of a moral principle we need only look to the *merely* probable. As long as we can find some support to justify a particular view, based on a well-reasoned position supported by a few biblical texts or one reputable authority, then such guidance can be safely followed even though it is a minority view.[1]

A good example to help illustrate the difference between these two approaches concerns the ethics of charging interest on loans. Based on the preponderance of biblical references, most from the Old Testament, and a widespread consensus among Christian thinkers (in addition to those in Judaism and Islam) up to the Reformation, we could argue that it is more probable that we should not charge interest on loans. By contrast, we could focus attention on what we have learned about the real nature of money, banking, and economies over time, and accept the theological rationale of John Calvin, which is supported by modern authorities. On this basis, we can make a case that charging a moderate rate of interest on loans to those who are in a position to repay is probably ethical from a Christian point of view. Like most issues in ethics, this question is complex, and deserves far more consideration than we have given it here.

Thus we have four ways of approaching the task of applying generic moral principles to particular circumstances. Generally speaking, the differences among the various approaches depend on the extent to which we give priority to either of two factors: the generic principle or the particular circumstance. The rigorist and laxist approaches mark the two extremes. The two middle positions, which focus on what is probable, have at least two things in common. Both reflect a greater awareness of the subtleties of moral analysis that can make adopting the rigorist and laxist approaches unacceptable. This is particularly true in circumstances where the discernment of moral principles seems to be difficult, or where more than one principle appears to be relevant to a particular situation.

Two things should be noticed here. First, even though we may usually seek to explore moral questions by using one of these four modes, nevertheless, as human beings we are still capable of being arbitrary and inconsistent. Second, even when we are conscientious, the process of weighing the meaning of moral principles and examining the particulars of circumstances may produce inconsistent results. Here are two examples. Thomas Aquinas is associated with a tradition of moral reasoning that often led to the production of handbooks of moral theology that were highly deductive in their approach, yet Aquinas himself urged caution when moving from general moral principles to increasingly specific rules for particular situations. He believed that the further we move down the chain of moral reasoning, from first principles to greater specificity, the more likely we are to be in error. This is because our thinking becomes more and more dependent on factors that are contextual and variable.[2]

A second example comes from Nathaniel Hawthorne's *The Scarlet Letter*. There we find a portrait of the Puritan town beadle, an official, we are told, who was responsible for administering the "whole dismal severity of the Puritanic code of law. . . in its final and closest application to the offender." Yet given that characterization of his role, he acts in a way we might not expect under the circumstances, applying the rules with a measure of leniency and causing comment among some of the bystanders.[3]

Scholars tell us that the Puritans were not as "puritanical" as we imagine. Nevertheless, what we assume to be their strict approach to community life is sometimes used to justify choosing other and more lenient ways of understanding the proper connection between moral principles and daily life. How do we steer a course between Puritan rigor and moral laxity? We need to recognize that every human community must deal with a common challenge: how we will respond to the gap between our ethical principles and the actual practice of our daily lives.

One of the more widely discussed General Convention resolutions in recent years was Resolution A104s/a, passed in 1991. The convention resolved "that this Church continue to work to reconcile the discontinuity between [the teaching of the Episcopal Church concerning human sexuality] and the experience of many members of this body." The same resolution also confessed "our failure to lead and to resolve this discontinuity through legislative efforts based on resolutions directed at singular and various aspects of these issues." The language of this resolution implies that such a discontinuity between teaching and experience is unusual, and that further efforts at legislative action might actually yield a different result. Perhaps it would be more realistic, however, as well as more consistent with our understanding of the fall and human sin, to expect ambiguity. This side of the New Jerusalem, there will always be some discontinuity between the moral principles embodied in church teaching and the actual experience of baptized members.

How do we address this apparent discontinuity between principles and practices in our community? One common way is to exclude the erring members: those who fail to embody the principles in their practice are threatened with expulsion from the community. If carried through consistently and absolutely, the community will inevitably shrink, given human nature and the continuing effects of the fall. Alternatively, we can address this gap between moral practice and moral principles by giving the benefit of the doubt to what we call the "realities" of daily life. By including and recognizing people's actual way of life, the number of commonly recognized principles will inevitably shrink. Principles that obviously cannot be lived out will be in danger of being jettisoned on the grounds of irrelevance or inappropriateness.

Clearly, we have sketched two extreme positions, and very few communities are likely to embody either approach fully. Whether we recognize it or not, most communities find themselves living in the gap between the principles that provide normative guidance and practices that fall short of full compliance. In this era, many Anglicans make a virtue of what we like to call our *via media* approach. With respect to moral theology and community life, I think this label provides a fair description. Our tradition tends to take the approach of an idealist or a purist when articulating the moral principles that are to shape our lives and communities, but when it comes to administering the structures and policies of our daily life and pastoral practice, we take a more gradualist approach. Recognizing the realism of Paul's words that "all have sinned and fall short of the glory of God" (Romans 3:23), we anticipate that all the baptized are on a journey of growth and sanctification through this world. We are not yet "there," at the point of fulfillment! When a community formally embraces this insight, it is able to recognize ambiguity in its midst. Inevitably members of the community will fail to embody and manifest the community's moral principles in their practice of daily life.

What do we make of this ambiguity? Do we extend the *via media* and make a virtue of "falling short"? Do we minimize the demands of our moral principles with the justification that we will always come up short, and say that what really counts is the attitude of our hearts? Or do we recognize the value of the growth and journey metaphors, seeing in them a con-

tinuing incentive to move forward toward our fulfillment and completion in Christ? An approach to moral
theology that values its deep bond with spirituality,
such as has been characteristic of the best of
Anglicanism, will always pursue the latter possibility.
We will not seek to justify our continuing failure to
embody our community's moral principles in our
daily lives.

A very good illustration of how this concept plays
a regular part in the life of our parishes is in our
approach to Christian marriage, and the question of
divorce and remarriage in the church. If you examine
the prayer book rite for The Celebration and Blessing
of a Marriage, there is no question about its theology:
Christian marriage is a life-long monogamous union
in God of a man and woman. The same point is made
in the Catechism, where we find the following words:
"Holy Matrimony is Christian marriage, in which the
woman and man enter into a life-long union, make
their vows before God and the Church, and receive the
grace and blessing of God to help them fulfill their
vows" (BCP 861). At the same time, we know from
our experience that we have canons permitting the
remarriage of divorced persons in church. It may be
tempting to see this as a contradiction, but the provi-
sion for remarriage can also be seen as an opportunity for a return to obedience rather than as a sanction
for sin.

Another reason why the daily moral practice of
Christians may not directly connect with the recognized moral principles of the community may be that
there is a need for change. This raises one of the most
challenging questions that any community will have
to face. Is this discontinuity part of the lingering
effects of the fall, or is it telling us that these principles need to be revised so as to "catch up with" the

actual life of the Spirit-led community and the prompting of God? When we find ourselves with no ready and clear answer to the question, two principles can help us explore the alternatives. The first is the principle of consensus and assurance that we have already explored in chapter two: the greater the demonstrable consensus in the praying community of the church as it reflects on scripture over the course of time, the greater our assurance that the view is in accord with God's will for us.

Second, just as is the case with Christian doctrine, the principles of moral theology that are received from the tradition enjoy the benefit of the doubt whenever they are challenged by new interpretations or proposals. While this second principle may seem confining to those who have a special vision for change, it is essential for maintaining the community with a coherent sense of order and continuity. This principle does not preclude the possibility of a change in our moral principles; it merely provides a guide for how change may best come about. Without a principle that gives the benefit of the doubt to what has been handed down, no common assumptions among members of the community can be assured. This may seem fine to some individuals, but those who depend upon fellowship and communication within a stable community will experience frustration and difficulty. This is especially true when what has been received is believed to have a divine origin.

∾ Love, Discernment, and Judgment

One of the most frequently quoted passages of scripture is Jesus' saying, "Do not judge, so that you may not be judged" (Matthew 7:1). It is usually quoted in situations where a person or group is admonished not to criticize the behavior of others. However, it is likely that the kinds of judgments that Jesus forbids are assessments of the final state of another's soul. Such judgments usurp God's role—for God is the only one who is in a position to make a final appraisal of the moral worth of another person. This is quite a different matter from using reason and reflection to assess the structure and moral character of acts that we witness on an everyday basis. For example, how could we faithfully seek to obey Jesus' saying about not judging unless we had a clear idea of what judging involves? The way that we arrive at such an idea is through reflective and reasoned analysis of our own actions and those of others. Such analysis helps us identify what Jesus specifically meant to forbid.

Perhaps you have heard this maxim: "Smart people learn from personal mistakes; wise people learn from the mistakes of others." There are many problems and troubles that we can avoid in life when we heed the advice of cautionary tales and observe the workings of cause and effect. For example, drivers' education programs often feature discussions of accident statistics and films of auto crashes as a way of encouraging discernment about actions and their consequences. Reference is made to the previous actions of others so that a new generation of drivers can be helped to avoid some of the same mistakes. Or consider courses about substance abuse that are usually a part of public school health curricula and ordination training programs. These courses are provided not only to those who seem to be at risk, but for all students so that they can recognize the kinds of behaviors that can lead them and others into a pattern of self-destruction. At the same time, the positive examples of others can also give us insight about choices that we can make in daily life. Consider what we learn from watching a story on the evening news about a neighborhood volunteer project for youth, or what we discover when a fellow employee invites us to join a work team on a Habitat for Humanity home. These kinds of experiences can lead us to see how the choice to serve others can enrich the lives of both the givers and the receivers of help. Though many of us now may find the practice quaint, reading the lives of the saints provides the same kind of opportunity to form a positive impression about choices and actions that lead to a growth in holiness.

When we hear stories and anecdotes, when we watch films or read novels, we engage in a process of reflective analysis about the actions of others and the decisions leading to them. Noting the significance of an action, and how its repetition contributes to the formation of virtue and vice, we learn to judge what kind of actions contribute to the good and what kind lead away from it. At the same time, by neglecting this moral analysis we can allow acts to shape our moral character as a result of our own indifference and inattention. Two collects in *The Book of Common Prayer* mention the kind of judgment we are exploring here. The Collect for Peace in Evening Prayer links the gift of right judgments with a focus upon doing God's will.

> Most holy God, the source of all good desires, all right judgments, and all just works: Give to us, your servants, that peace which the world cannot give, so that our minds may be fixed on the doing of your will, and that we, being delivered from the fear of all enemies, may live in peace and quietness; through the mercies of Christ Jesus our Savior. (BCP 123)

Another collect develops the same idea by referring to the process of discernment between true and false choices, as we seek to follow our Lord and walk in love.

> O God, by whom the meek are guided in judg-
> ment, and light riseth up in darkness for the
> godly: Grant us, in all our doubts and uncer-
> tainties, the grace to ask what thou wouldest
> have us to do, that the Spirit of wisdom may
> save us from all false choices, and that in thy
> light we may see light, and in thy straight path
> may not stumble; through Jesus Christ our
> Lord. (BCP 832)

Discernment and judgment are gifts given to us so that we may be able to choose and act well. Like all gifts, they can be used as the giver intends or not. To notice that a friend seems headed for trouble because of a long-standing pattern of thoughtless living can lead us to do a number of things. The first is to learn what we can from his example; the second is to decide if and how we are going to continue to relate to him. Here Jesus' words about judging have their special relevance. Let us assume that the choices this friend makes are not a danger to us, but do evoke our moral disapproval. The hardest thing we are called to do in this situation is not to cut ourselves off from him, comforting ourselves with the thought that our friend's behavior warrants a separation. To believe that our relationship with him is beyond redemption because of his behavior is to have made a judgment about *him,* and not simply about his conduct. In effect, we have condemned him. We are called "to represent Christ and his Church; to bear witness to him wherever" we may be, and "to carry on Christ's work of reconciliation in the world" (BCP 855). Our refusal of fellowship with those of whom we disapprove may imply something negative about Christ's relationship with them now and in eternity.

Jesus warns us about actions that represent our final judgment of others. At the same time, if we are to be obedient followers, we need to make reasonable acts of discernment about the nature of moral actions. We should notice why such discernment is important. As we have seen, acts of conscience involve a mixture of reason, feelings, and other facets of moral subjectivity, so the connections we make between moral principles and particular circumstances is always open to analysis. There is a real difference between reflecting on human conduct to discover what moral principles mean in action, and doing it in order to condemn others for their behavior. We may conclude that the risk of condemnation is so great that we must simply give up on decisions about the moral value of other people's actions, but if we do, it will be the first step in fooling ourselves. We are constantly learning from reflection upon our own actions and those of others as we pass through each day and week. The real issue is what we do with this insight. Do we use it to justify ourselves and condemn others? Or do we use this learning to promote our own moral growth and to help us fulfill the mission of the church "to restore all people to unity with God and each other in Christ" (BCP 855)?

⋘ The Meanings of an Act

Our hesitancy about judging others may have another source, too; it may have to do with our understanding of the meaning of action. In chapter three we discussed the question of moral value, asking whether values can be found only in people's thinking, or in their behavior and actions as well. Sometimes we refuse to judge the moral value of another person's action because we suspect that it is hidden from us, wholly private to another person and his or her intentions. But do intentions entirely shape the moral value of our actions? We should hesitate about saying yes to this question, because our acts have more than one meaning.

For example, imagine that someone behind the wheel of a car is preoccupied by several unfinished tasks. Flashing lights in the rearview mirror startle the driver, who immediately looks down at the speedometer and sees he is going well above the speed limit. Rolling down the window, he stammers, "Officer, I really meant to be going only fifty-five." However foolish it sounds, he is sincere. At least in this situation, the driver believes that his good intention is the primary meaning of the act, but it should not surprise us to discover that the highway patrol officer might take a different view.

In addition to the meaning that we intend for our acts—what we might call the *intentional* meaning—we can acknowledge another. Many of the things we do have a commonly understood meaning in the eyes of others, what we might call the *generic* meaning of our acts. Suppose that I am at home spending a day off doing some yard work. I find that my rake is broken. Looking across the street to the home of my new neighbors, I see the garage door open even though the cars are gone. I decide that I will borrow a rake from the other garage. Since the neighbors are not home, I am not able to ask permission. Now suppose I am seen carrying the rake back to my house by another neighbor. I may think of myself as temporarily borrowing the rake, but the neighbor who sees me take it might come to a different conclusion.

A third meaning of our acts often provides a different sort of self-justification, especially when we feel guilty about what we have done. What results from our actions, despite our intentions and what others conclude about them, also gives them meaning. Therefore, when things come to a good result even after we have acted poorly, we like to point to how things turned out. We call this the *consequential* meaning of our acts. When we assert that "the end does not justify the means," we are talking about the consequential meaning of our acts being stressed at the expense of their other meanings. By the same token, when we believe that we have made a well-reasoned choice and have acted for the good, we can still be troubled by unexpected negative consequences of our action. For example, a teacher may discern the special gifts of a musical child and tell the parents about a scholarship for summer music camp. If the teacher writes a recommendation that helps the child win a scholarship, and if the child then suffers an unfortunate accident while away, the teacher may feel responsible.

The potential disparity between these three meanings of our acts is frequently the source of both humor and drama in books and films. What we intend and what we fail to consider as we shape our acts may be very different from what is important to others, who both respond to our acts and shape their own. As if the potential disparity between different meanings of our acts were not complex enough, there is one more variable. When we remember the difference between laws, manners, and moral principles, we are in a better position to appreciate why reflecting on past moral acts and thinking about future acts can be a very challenging process. As the movie *The Fugitive* showed us, we can intend to act for the sake of the moral good and still break the law. At the same time, despite both our own intentions and what others may think, the things we do may bring about both good and evil results. A well-known story in the gospels shows how the different meanings of our acts can diverge. Jesus notes the irony of Judas using a common form of social greeting as a means by which to achieve his betrayal: "Judas, would you betray the Son of Man with a kiss?" (Luke 22:48, NEB). And as we learn from the biblical text and Christian doctrine, Judas' act had a variety of consequences for him, for the disciples, and for the subsequent history of the world.

～ Axioms for Moral Theology

17. Conscience both discerns generic moral principles, and applies them to particular circumstances. The act of applying generic principles to particular situations is called casuistry.

18. Moral principles, norms, or rules are always generic, even when they become more and more specific; they must still be individually applied to particular situations. No matter how specific moral principles or rules become, we must still engage in a personal exercise of conscience.

19. Anglican moral theology has tended to take the approach of an idealist or a purist at the level of principle, and a gradualist approach at the level of policy and practice in the church's pastoral life. We should not water down the claims of the gospel upon us, while we should remember that Christian life involves stages of growth.

20. Principles of moral theology that are received from the tradition enjoy the benefit of the doubt when challenged by new interpretations or proposals. This does not preclude change; it only guides how change must come about if we are to honor the good of public order in our communities.

21. If the articulation of Christian ethics is limited to particular situations, it risks being based on something less than a full range of moral principles. When we focus on particular situations, we must remember to ask what *kinds* of circumstances these situations exemplify.

Chapter Eight

Building a Case in Christian Ethics

Keep, O Lord, your household the Church in your steadfast faith and love, that through your grace we may proclaim your truth with boldness, and minister your justice with compassion; for the sake of our Savior Jesus Christ, who lives and reigns with you and the Holy Spirit, one God, now and for ever. (BCP 230)

Heated debate about moral issues has become such a common experience for many of us that we can be forgiven for wondering if there is any future for a positive exploration of ethical questions in the Christian community. We may be pessimistic and think that consensus about moral issues is beyond the realm of possibility for any group of human beings this side of Eden, regardless of the power of the resurrection. Shall we surrender all hope for corporate study and discussion of ethical questions? Shall we give up on the search for a common mind and a common heart about how we should respond to the concerns that shape our daily lives? I hope not! I have written this book because I do believe there is a viable Anglican approach to moral theology. Throughout I have presented some of the basic principles and concepts that form the building blocks for such an approach. Much more can and should be said, but there is enough here to help anyone get started down the path of thinking more effectively about issues in moral theology.

Before we proceed, it may help to remember a theme from earlier chapters: we do not live the moral life alone. As baptized Christians, we are members of the body of Christ, a community whose unity is rooted in him. The rite for Holy Baptism reminds us that

> There is one Body and one Spirit;
> There is one hope in God's call to us;
> One Lord, one Faith, one Baptism;
> One God and Father of all. (BCP 299)

These sweeping statements are true for very diverse and unique individuals. We need to have confidence that there is one common pattern of response to God's call to us, and we discover it in a common moral life that is a gift from the hand of our one God and Father to his many and varied children. There is surely a meaningful path we can describe and follow that runs between the impenetrable forest of uniform regulations and the open swamp of formless indifference. We may rightly fear a cookie-cutter approach to the moral life that disregards individuality and the dignity of personal conscience, but we should not let such a fear convince us that the only alternative for our public discussion and teaching is an unprincipled relativism. We can and should look for common principles embodied in a wisdom that is shared among members of the community. As we do, we can remember that having common principles does not imply one particular structure of governance or discipline.

As members of the church, how shall we approach moral questions that arise in daily life? Where will we discern a body of principles to form the shared wisdom for our community? My goal in this chapter is to introduce you to a method for addressing ethical issues, a basic approach taken by most reference works in ethics and theology and appropriate for use by individuals, parish study groups, diocesan ethics committees, and national church commissions. Because what we need to ask and learn in all of these contexts is at heart the same, a common method is best for responding to ethical questions and presenting a compelling case.

One of our basic axioms for moral theology is that Anglicans look for a consensus in coming to agreement about the pattern of a life that is worthy of the calling. The most secure beliefs in Christian theology are those that fulfill the Vincentian Canon: they have been everywhere believed by all persons at all times. This does not mean that Anglicans have a checklist of acceptable beliefs and practices that literally meet these criteria. Yet when a belief is consistent with the teaching of scripture and appears to have been affirmed by the greater part of the Christian community throughout the world over the course of the centuries, it provides us with greater assurance that it reflects God's will for us. Let us also remember that such assurance is never a guarantee, and is always a matter of greater or lesser, never an either/or. Thus the method I am offering here will help us build a more compelling case in order to provide greater assurance for the conclusions at which we arrive.

There are at least two reasons why we need a clear and common method for sorting out moral questions and issues. First, our approach to ethics will have more integrity if we are consistent in our approach. For example, without good reason we cannot treat questions about money and material goods differently from the way we treat questions about marriage and human sexuality. We should not stress biblical principles when addressing one set of issues but ignore them when addressing another. Second, Anglicans have no institutional magisterium or authoritative text that will answer all moral questions for us; neither the resolutions of Lambeth Conference nor those of General Convention can provide such definitive teaching. Instead, Anglicans need to build a case, and we need a clear and easily employed method that will help us shape what we believe are adequate and appropriate responses to ethical questions.

To illustrate this method, I will choose an issue that I have referred to several times already: Is it ever appropriate for a baptized Christian to be associated with acts of violence? For most of us, ethical questions arise in connection with actual choices that we have to make, and one example from an earlier chapter concerns an eighteen-year-old high school graduate who asks herself, "Is it right for me, as a baptized Christian, to enlist in the army?" This same question could also be pursued in a generic way. Perhaps the young woman is part of a parish study group meeting over the course of the autumn to reflect on the broader question of Christian participation in military service.

There is a difference between questions about particular cases, like "What should I do here and now?", and questions that are generic, like "Is it right for someone to do such and such?" The first question has other factors bound up with it, such as personal vocation, responsibility to one's own family, and previous commitments. For example, one might believe that it is right for Christians in general to enlist, but that it is not right for me to do so because God has other plans for me. Nevertheless, someone asking the personal and particular question will inevitably raise the generic question, and members of a study group pondering the generic question will tend to consider particular cases as well. Such a study group plays a very important role with respect to ethical questions precisely because it is in a better position to see beyond the personal factors that can make asking ethical questions so difficult for most of us. Nevertheless, as we observed with respect to the idea of conscience, the work of study groups and commissions does not replace the need for each of us to seek insights about generic principles and apply them to our own circumstances.

The method that I am recommending for use in approaching ethical issues is very simple in its structure, although it can be as complex and lengthy a task as we care to make it. It has three basic steps: (1) to identify and clarify the topic; (2) to analyze and reflect on the resources we need in order to explore the topic; and (3) to generalize and come to conclusions. Another way to remember the steps is through the letters I, A, and G: *identify, analyze,* and *generalize.* Identification is the process of seeking to discern everything related to the topic at hand, and is best done by brainstorming. Analysis moves from this open-ended activity to a kind of sorting process. We stand back from the data at hand and try to notice order, patterns, and relationships among the data. With the third step, generalization, we synthesize what we have learned from analysis and try to state clearly the conclusions we have reached.

How does this method work out in practice? Let's say we are trying to reach a decision about the use of handguns. First we will ask, "What other questions could possibly relate to it?" Brainstorming a list of related questions might produce the following. "Does it make a difference if a handgun is concealed or not? Is carrying a handgun ethically different from carrying a shotgun for duck hunting? Is it right for police officers to carry handguns even though ordinary citizens cannot?" After brainstorming has produced for us a list of related questions, in step two we begin to analyze the list looking for common denominators and patterns. Thus we might identify authority, community, and justice as significant themes to be explored in connection with the question of handguns. Finally we are ready to generalize. Perhaps we started with the initial question, "Is it appropriate for me to carry a handgun?" Generalizing from the analysis we did in step two, we can choose to ask a broader question: "Is it ever appropriate for a Christian to engage in an act of violence?" This broader question may provide more scope for the exploration of some important themes, including the significance of community authority and the value of maintaining community justice. Considering such factors might lead to a distinction between degrees of moral justification for particular actions. One might, for example, build a case for how some, but not all, baptized persons might carry handguns with the morally appropriate intention of using them in some specific circumstances.

These are the steps we need to follow in order to build a case. When we start to read and investigate, we will notice that for most ethical questions, earlier thinkers and writers have done considerable work before us and with research and study we can learn from them. It is also likely that those who have asked these questions before us have also made a case for certain conclusions. When we can begin to gather a consensus for the conclusions at which we and others have arrived, then we are on the road to finding the kind of assurance we need that our ethical reasoning is Spirit-led.

~ Step One: Identifying and Clarifying the Topic

The most effective starting point for approaching a question or issue in ethics is to identify and clarify the question. What is being asked? What else do we need to ask? What other questions are involved? A high school graduate's question about her own possible enlistment, a parish study group exploring the same question in a more general way, a young man considering an assignment on a submarine carrying nuclear missiles, and the Mary and Martha Guild's question about the appropriateness of carrying handguns all have a common root. Is it ever right for Christians to engage in an act of violence? When we encounter a question like this in ethics, it is helpful to pause and consider what is being asked before trying to respond.

For example, Christian ethicists in the long tradition before us have noticed that the use of knives to cause wounds, the loss of limbs, and even death does not necessarily mean the knives were used in inappropriate acts of violence. Both members of street gangs and surgeons in the operating room can use knives "violently" on human tissue, causing wounds that involve bleeding and bruising as well as pain. Yet the gang member and the surgeon are involved in very different kinds of actions. This should help us see that when asking ethical questions about human relations and the possibility of conflict, we have to consider the meanings we attach to words like force and violence. We should also notice the difference that factors like intention can make in the structure of moral action.

Another way of clarifying a question in ethics is to consider the way in which it is related to other questions that could be asked. If I am trying to come to some clarity about the moral value of using nuclear weapons, I might also ask how this question may be related to questions about the use of violent weapons in other eras, such as why crossbows were prohibited at one point in the Middle Ages. I may come to see that at very different points in history, Christians who could morally justify involvement in some acts of violence have nevertheless concluded that the use of certain weapons is morally prohibited for one common reason: the disproportionate damage that these weapons can cause.

The same process of identification through brainstorming can be used with questions having to do with economics, the uses of medicine, and the nature of human sexuality. Moving too quickly to consider a particular question before seeing what might be involved in asking it can close off potential insights and avenues of discovery. Asking broader or more general questions will probably give us a more encompassing view, even if we do not see their immediate relevance in all the areas of our inquiry.

⟿ Step Two: Analyzing and Reflecting on Resources and Materials

Now we turn to analysis and study. Can someone with no particular theological training who lives far from a good library make these discoveries? It may seem that I am advocating an approach to moral issues that is really only suitable for a diocesan or national study commission with formal training and resources. Actually, just about everyone can use this method with a few basic resources. You will need a good study Bible, along with *The Oxford Companion to the Bible* and a one-volume biblical commentary such as the *New Jerome Bible Commentary; The Book of Common Prayer; The Oxford Dictionary of the Christian Church;* and a reference volume like *The Westminster Dictionary of Christian Ethics* or *The New Dictionary of Christian Ethics and Pastoral Theology.* Most dioceses have resource centers and retreat and conference centers where such books can be found. For those with access to the Internet, a solid resource is Britannica Online (www.eb.com), which makes available the latest edition of the *Encyclopedia Britannica.* Try looking up topics like "just war principles," "pacifism," and "violence."

This second step of analysis and reflection upon resources and materials from throughout the Christian tradition is the main thing we need to do in order to respond in an adequate and appropriate way to questions in Christian ethics. We need to begin by examining the biblical material, and we will be on firm ground if we use the Old Testament, the Apocrypha, and the New Testament in the widest possible way.

For example, in looking at the Old Testament, we will not want to confine our identification of texts to the sixth commandment and to other laws or rules that directly pertain to conflict and violence. If we did, we would miss what might be gained from at least two other important sources within this part of the Bible. The historical books (particularly 1 and 2 Samuel and 1 and 2 Kings) present many stories about conflict between individuals and nations, and perceptions about God's will for those who are involved. One example is Saul's failure to follow God's command to destroy the Amalekites and spare no one—not even their animals. Saul's neglect of the commandment causes God to reject him as king (1 Samuel 15).

Another example comes from the prophetic books, which provide another important source of learning. One text that deals with war and peace is the prophet Isaiah's conversation with King Ahaz of Judah when Jerusalem was under attack from the northern kingdom of Israel. God sends Isaiah to reassure the king that the Davidic monarchy will continue and that his true security lies in the Lord, not in the possession of large armies or great weapons (Isaiah 7:1-9). At that point we may want to turn to John's account of Jesus' overthrow of the money changers and cleansing of the temple with "a whip of cords" (John 2:15), which in this gospel is one of Jesus' first public acts. The theme of violence and the threat of violence in the story can be read in a variety of ways. When we notice and reflect upon the issues involved in each of these and many similar texts, we can see how quick and simple answers fail to do justice to what turn out to be complex questions. Throughout the Bible, we will want to be attentive to the variety of texts from which we can gain theological insight about God's will for us as we contemplate these questions.

If we begin our search for relevant resources and materials by focusing on the Bible, and if we use several resource books, we can get some assistance in our identification of significant texts. One particularly helpful book is Richard Hays's *The Moral Vision of the New Testament*, where the author identifies and discusses many key biblical passages. Starting with a large newsprint pad, or several blank pages in a notebook, we can begin by simply listing texts that we think *might* be relevant. We can save sorting them for the next step of analysis. You might try this yourself, with a few members of your mission or parish, or your study group. See if you come up with similar lists of texts, and if the resource volumes that you

consult recommend the same texts as being relevant
to the topic of violence, war, and peace. If we agree
that no single effort in this direction is likely to be
definitive, then any attempt we make at the task can
be improved upon, often through comparison with
the efforts of others.

Whether you use a book like Hays's or a one-volume biblical commentary such as the *New Jerome Bible
Commentary* or *The International Bible Commentary*,
with time you will become more familiar with the his-
torical-critical and literary-critical forms of biblical
scholarship. These are the kinds of study methods that
help us to see, for example, that the text from 1
Samuel referred to above is one of at least two different accounts of why Saul and his line were replaced
from kingship. Following up such an insight with the
help of the *New Oxford Annotated Bible* or similar
study Bible, you will find out about the concept of
Holy War, an idea we also read about in our newspapers. When we investigate an idea like this, as well as
others in the Old Testament, we can gain a better
appreciation for the significance of other New
Testament texts, such as the story of Jesus' entry into
Jerusalem. We are told that he rode into the city on a
donkey, whereas the arrival of one publicly proclaimed as a king riding on a horse would have pro-
jected the image of a warrior. Furthermore,
acquaintance with various types of texts and ideas in
the Old Testament can help provide insight about the
way in which Jesus and the New Testament writers
appropriated, adapted, or rejected themes and images
from the tradition before them. Jesus' words about
the "eye for an eye" rule in the Sermon on the Mount
(Exodus 21:23-24) provide a good example.

When we turn from the Bible to Christian history
in our research on Christian attitudes to violence,

there is a wealth of material from the patristic, medieval, Reformation, and contemporary periods. Reference to theological contributions from the eastern sphere of Christianity would enhance this sort of survey, but will not fall neatly into these historical divisions because of the differences in social and cultural traditions. With regard to violence, we can discern two predominant but contrasting stances from the biblical period right up to the present. In almost every age, many sincere and thoughtful Christians have felt called to renounce any involvement with violent acts, while others have come to the conclusion that under certain circumstances violent acts could serve the cause of justice and love. In organizing our historical and contemporary materials for analysis and reflection, we can gather all the materials within each period and study each one separately. Or we could draw up two historical time-lines from the Bible to the present day, one detailing the views of those who have been opposed to violence in any form, and the other tracing the view that violence is permissible under specific circumstances. I tend to favor the former approach, which allows for a more encompassing view of each period before moving to the next.

In the early church, baptismal instruction often called upon candidates to leave certain walks of life, among them the career of soldier in the Roman army. There are different reasons why this was the case. For instance, soldiering required oaths to pagan deities. In late antiquity, Augustine of Hippo made a significant contribution to Christian reflection upon the meaning of Jesus' command to love another when faced with the prospect of involvement in acts of violence. You will want to discover on what grounds he could suggest that we refrain from defending ourselves yet still defend others from the threat of violence.

In the medieval period, we can explore the three principles articulated by Thomas Aquinas according to which an act of violence or war might be considered an act of justice. Here we will want to notice the purpose of the criteria: not to determine if war itself is just, but rather to determine if acts of war on this or that occasion may be defended as serving justice. His near-contemporaries were the Franciscans, whose founder is often credited with emphasizing a very different approach to the question of violence and the good of peace. A study of views in this period would also be strengthened by reference to the various church canons that sought to limit the involvement of ordained persons in acts of war.

A rich resource of the Reformation period is Martin Luther's theology of the two kingdoms, providing some justification for a distinction between worldly and spiritual conduct. Calvin's concept of the "third use of the law," which envisions a positive role for law in Christian community, provides an interesting contrast with traditional Lutheran views. Both need to be considered in relation to the maintenance of civil order and the question of the use of force. These can be compared with the beliefs of various Anabaptist communities from the same period who are associated with pacifism and with sectarian withdrawal from the society around them. The Roman Catholic tradition in the period of the Counter-Reformation continued to reflect on questions of war and violence; the name of Francesco Suarez is associated with three criteria for deciding whether certain practices in the conduct of war might serve the good of justice. Pursuing this sort of a study, furthermore, will reveal how a number of the ideas associated with the contributions of these various persons from the Reformation period directly influenced the thinking of Christians in Europe and North America at the time of the Second World War.

When we pursue a survey of various historical periods in the Christian tradition, it is often helpful if we give some attention to the example of particular individuals, especially those Christians who have not left specific writings behind explaining or seeking to justify their views. For example, while most Christians prior to the time of Constantine appear to have found military service inconsistent with Christian practice, that changed after the emperor's conversion. No longer a persecuted minority in a hostile religious and political climate, Christians were part of the official religion of the realm. Those who once may have faced being dragged before magistrates subsequently found themselves serving as magistrates. Praying for peace in a hostile environment takes on new meaning when one comes to have some official responsibility for the maintenance of that peace.

Anglican reflection on the question of association with acts of violence has been invariably shaped by the fact that Anglicanism has its source in an established church. There are Anglicans who believe that acts of war cannot be justified but are nevertheless ambivalent about abandoning an armed police force to maintain peace and civil order in our own communities. It will help us to learn what we can about Anglican thought given to this question from the sixteenth century to the present. Some interesting examples are provided by the military experience of two Anglican clergy. Leonides Polk, a bishop of Louisiana, and a saintly English priest called Hugh Lister both served as commanding officers in wartime. Polk served on the battlefield as a general in the Confederate Army during the Civil War; Lister, although a pacifist, signed up for a command in a World War II combat unit and died on the front lines in Belgium. Neither one, to my knowledge, left any explanation of the ethics of his decision to serve, but they are examples to be considered alongside a cleric whose views are better known, the pacifist Bishop Paul Jones of Utah, whom we commemorate on our calendar of Lesser Feasts. The twentieth-century English theologian Charles Raven was also a pacifist whose views made him the object of criticism at a time of popular support for involvement in war. We should also remember that the Episcopal Church has a Bishop for the Armed Forces and many chaplains in military service; at the same time, many Episcopalians have been active in protest movements against the Vietnam and Gulf Wars. Other Christians have wrestled with these issues in terms of a personal vocation to the police force as well as the armed forces, and given significant thought to the decision of whether or not to serve in a time of war.

Resolutions and documents from the Lambeth Conferences and the many General Conventions of the Episcopal Church are a good source of Anglican views about the issue of violence, the maintenance of civil order, war, and the pursuit of peace. Most notable is the 1930 Lambeth Conference Resolution 25, which has been reaffirmed at every subsequent conference. It states that "war as a method of settling international disputes is incompatible with the teaching and example of our Lord Jesus Christ."[1]

This kind of historical survey is not really possible with contemporary issues like medical ethics or ecology. But although these questions are definitely contemporary problems, they are still related to questions of a more general nature that Christians have considered for centuries. Any discussion of organ transplantation, for example, would be enhanced by studying

what the Christian tradition has to say about caring
for the sick, as well as what we can find out about the
history of medicine and its purposes. We can look at
the principles behind the Hippocratic Oath, which is
associated with the name and practice of an ancient
Greek physician and continues to shape medical practice today. Another feature of modern life we can
investigate ethically concerns the way that technolog-
ical developments have blurred the distinctions
between questions that were formerly separate. For
example, the ethics of violence and the ethics of medicine intersect in morally significant ways, and we
often depend on moral description to distinguish
them. Is an act of abortion an act of medicine for the
mother and/or an act of violence against the unborn?
Should a society that mandates capital punishment
for certain crimes allow a method of execution—lethal
injection—to be virtually indistinguishable in the
minds of most people from euthanasia, which some
would describe as a medical practice? Looking at the
question historically does not provide an immediate
answer, but it can help us to think more effectively
about some of these complex distinctions.

⁓ **Step Three: Generalizing and Coming
to Some Conclusions**
Reflecting on the survey that I have described above
may easily lead us to think that investigating the historical background to ethical questions is beyond
most of us. This is understandable, but I think that we
arrive at such a conclusion because of a misleading
assumption: that each of us needs to have a definitive
view about most questions in ethics. It is true that
each of us must make choices in daily life, and quite
often we do not have the luxury of time to study,
think, and reflect upon various principles that might

shape our decisions. Nevertheless, we are Christians who live in community, whose theology and spirituality is formed and shaped in community. That is why ethical questions are best explored in a generic way by groups of interested persons who can share their learning and their various points of view. If we find it hard to arrive at conclusions about difficult ethical questions, it may be that we need to go back to reading, reflection, prayer, and conversation with others who have worked on the issues that we are exploring. Learning from and summarizing the conclusions of others will lead us to greater clarity of mind.

In step three we try to draw some general conclusions about what our study has told us. We ask the questions: "Where do we find consensus? Where do we find a convergence of views in our tradition?" One good way to discern this is to ask two questions from the survey material we have gathered: "What is this person or group wishing to affirm, and what do they want to deny?" Often people who do not appear to agree in terms of their conclusions share similar assumptions and may wish to affirm the same things. Here is one example. When we investigate the Christian tradition of reflection on acts of violence and war, we find two dominant strains of response. A sizeable number of Christians have believed that no justification for such acts is possible; a sizeable number have believed otherwise. Leaving the matter there, we might simply conclude that there are two predominant and opposed views and either might be equally viable.

Yet we can probe a bit further by looking at what various individuals and groups have wanted to affirm. Theologians associated with the so-called just war theory do not necessarily imagine that acts of violence and war are good or inherently just things.

They may in fact share a central conviction with those who believe that Christians should never be involved in acts of violence, that peace should always be our goal and highest aim. Furthermore, they may even share with Christian pacifists a belief that war always involves evil effects upon persons and the world. The two viewpoints, therefore, are not polar opposites. We do not have to choose between believing that acts of violence are never justified or believing that they are always justified. Instead, it is a much narrower choice between believing that violence is never justified, and believing that violence might serve justice and the pursuit of peace on particular occasions and according to well-defined principles.

The point here is not to try and reconcile two ultimately different approaches, but to try to discern the nature of the difference and arrive at some generalizations and conclusions that may be helpful to us. We may be able to see more points of convergence than we had previously recognized between differing views, and to be more articulate about the nature of those differences. This can help us to shape the kind of case that others might find more compelling, and enable us to generate a greater consensus among members of the Christian community. While recognizing some areas of divergence within the tradition, we may also be able to show which authorities and resources have had the most influence on the tradition, and which ought to call later parts of the tradition to account. When we are looking at questions in some other areas of Christian ethics, we may find that with some issues there is a more evident consensus across the span of centuries than is the case with violence and peace. The most important thing that we can do with any issue is to take the time to probe the resources and be intellectually honest about what we find.

⮑ Conclusion

As we seek to make decisions for how to live today, we need to exercise the virtue of prudence. Doing moral theology presents us with the opportunity to develop and exercise prudence, which is the virtue of practical reason. Practical reason concerns itself with action. When we think about how we shall act for the good, and when we think about how we should act, we practice *prudential reasoning*. More specifically, we are engaged in this same type of reasoning when we think and reflect on moral principles as we pursue the process of discernment, and when we apply them to particular circumstances. Prudence is both developed and expressed in our action as we carry out the method I have described in this chapter. It plays a significant role in the way that we reflect on and consider the views of theologians who have lived before us as well as those of our contemporaries.

The search for an adequate and appropriate response to a moral question can be a humbling process, as many of us discover in our life in the church. Anyone can respond simply on impulse, without thought or reflection, but it takes prudence, wisdom, and patience to defer to the work of Christians who have gone before us in thinking, talking, and praying about some of the most challenging questions that life in this world presents. In more than one sense, we literally do not have all the answers. Quite often, we do not fully understand the questions that we find ourselves and our neighbors asking. As Anglicans, we do not have a rule book, a compendium of moral teachings that will answer every question or tell us the right thing to do in every situation. Yet we can still have faithful confidence. We have rich and substantive resources that will teach us if we open ourselves to them. We have the gift of God's ordered creation, the divinely inspired scriptures, and a long tradition of theological reflection based upon and shaped by them. We also have a rich tradition of speculative theological thinking and insights gained from the natural and social sciences. As we can learn from our study of the tradition, it is possible for both individuals and communities to err in their discernment and articulation of theological truth. Yet, it is also possible for the God-enabled, Christ-indwelled, and Spirit-led community to grow further and further into the fullness of the Risen Lord and his truth. As we seek moral wisdom and discernment, let us as a church seek to embody the words of the English poet Christopher Smart, which now form part of hymn 241:

> Take from him what ye will give him,
> of his fullness grace for grace;
> strive to think him, speak him, live him,
> till you find him face to face.

᪖ Axioms for Moral Theology

22. Anglican moral theology is most compelling when it seeks to build a case for a particular approach to an ethical question or issue. We can seek to commend an existing consensus for an approach to an issue or, through reasoned persuasion, we can seek to establish such a consensus where one does not yet exist.

Axioms for Moral Theology

1. Moral theology is about a life of holiness. After baptism, we seek to walk "in holiness and righteousness all our days." In moral theology we seek to describe and commend a life worthy of our calling. *(chapter 1)*

2. Moral theology is properly considered under the heading of sanctification, not justification. It is part of our walk from the font. Doing good will not save us; we do the good because we have been saved. *(chapter 1)*

3. Moral theology is not the same thing as, but is intimately related to, pastoral care. Moral theology begins with the consideration of generic principles; pastoral care begins with the consideration of a particular situation. *(chapter 1)*

4. Church conventions and other legislative gatherings do not "make" the church's moral theology. Instead, they face the challenge of

applying its moral principles to community legislation and discipline. *(chapter 1)*

5. Moral theology has two primary reference points: creation and scripture. Moral theology looks both to the world and our experience of life together within it, and to scripture and our tradition of reasoned reflection based upon it, as sources of moral principles. *(chapter 2)*

6. Moral theology works in light of an understanding of the four principal phases of salvation history: creation, fall, redemption, and the end of all things in Christ. *(chapter 2)*

7. In coming to agreement concerning the pattern of life that is worthy of the calling, Anglicans have looked for consensus. We have the greatest degree of assurance for what has been most widely received. *(chapter 2)*

8. Anglicans have looked for consensus in several interrelated spheres: the praying community of the church throughout the world; the wider community of the Body of Christ through history; and the academic community, when its work is founded upon Christian principles. *(chapter 2)*

9. All people, whether they are Christian or not, can receive moral knowledge through the "general revelation" of the Book of Nature. This is not to say that all people will do so, or that they will choose to act on such knowledge. *(chapter 3)*

10. Anglicans distinguish between moral knowledge, which is revealed to everyone through the Book of Nature, and saving knowledge, which is mediated through the "special revelation" of the Book of Scripture. Saving knowledge shapes life after baptism in such a way as to leave both continuity and discontinuity between the moral knowledge possessed by Christians and that of other people and traditions. *(chapter 4)*

11. The church may adopt one of two postures concerning the relationship between the gospel and the world: it may hold the world up to judgment, or it may witness to the gospel under whose judgment it also stands. *(chapter 5)*

12. The church speaks best to moral principles when it speaks about them descriptively rather than prescriptively. Describing the moral good invites others to discover its beauty; prescribing the moral good may cause others to feel defensive and suspect us of hypocrisy. *(chapter 5)*

13. Commonly held principles may nevertheless give rise to differing implementations in terms of policy and practice. Just because we agree on our principles does not mean we will agree on how we should live them. *(chapter 5)*

14. Acts shape character, and character shapes acts. Character is the disposition to act in particular ways. Individual acts are the building blocks of habits, and habits are the material of dispositions to act in particular ways. *(chapter 6)*

15. As a gift of creation, all people share a basic disposition to seek the good, but as a result of the fall we seek to rule ourselves. These basic dispositions give rise to the specific dispositions we call the natural moral virtues and the vices that shape moral action. *(chapter 6)*

16. Moral conscience involves the whole person, both thinking and feeling. It also involves the interrelated acts of reflection upon, and deliberation toward, moral action. Conscience must be followed, but conscience must also be educated. *(chapter 6)*

17. Conscience both discerns generic moral principles, and applies them to particular circumstances. The act of applying generic principles to particular situations is called casuistry. *(chapter 7)*

18. Moral principles, norms, or rules are always generic, even when they become more and more specific; they must still be individually applied to particular situations. No matter how specific moral principles or rules become, we must still engage in a personal exercise of conscience. *(chapter 7)*

19. Anglican moral theology has tended to take the approach of an idealist or a purist at the level of principle, and a gradualist approach at the level of policy and practice in the church's pastoral life. We should not water down the claims of the gospel upon us, while we should remember that Christian life involves stages of growth. *(chapter 7)*

20. Principles of moral theology that are received from the tradition enjoy the benefit of the doubt when challenged by new interpretations or proposals. This does not preclude change; it only guides how change must come about if we are to honor the good of public order in our communities. *(chapter 7)*

21. If the articulation of Christian ethics is limited to particular situations, it risks being based on something less than a full range of moral principles. When we focus on particular situations, we must remember to ask what *kinds* of circumstances these situations exemplify. *(chapter 7)*

22. Anglican moral theology is most compelling when it seeks to build a case for a particular approach to an ethical question or issue. We can seek to commend an existing consensus for an approach to an issue or, through reasoned persuasion, we can seek to establish such a consensus where one does not yet exist. *(chapter 8)*

Endnotes

Chapter 1: The Walk from the Font

1. *The Book of Common Prayer*, 223. Hereafter references will be cited in the text as BCP.

2. Kenneth E. Kirk, *The Vision of God: The Christian Doctrine of the Summum Bonum* (London, New York, Toronto: Longmans, Green & Co., 1931), ix-x.

3. Adapted from the familiar traditional translation, "The glory of God is a living man; and the life of man is the vision of God." Irenaeus, *Against Heresy* 4.20.6.

4. Augustine, *City of God*, 14.28.

5. Ronald Lawler, Jospeh Boyle, and William E. May, *Catholic Sexual Ethics* (Huntington, Ind.: Our Sunday Visitor, 1985), 66; emphasis added.

Chapter 2: Seeking to Live a Good Life

1. From a sixth-century Latin text in Hymn 59, and a text by Kathleen Thomerson found in Hymn 490, *The Hymnal 1982* (New York: Church Hymnal Corporation, 1985).

2. Words attributed to Richard of Chichester, and part of the text for Hymn 654 in *The Hymnal 1982*.

3. I am indebted to Professor Hud Hudson of the philosophy department at Western Washington University for suggestions and for helping me to avoid some philo-

sophically problematic ways of presenting a general definition of ethics.

4. See also BCP 324.

5. See the presentation of the Ten Commandments in the Catechism, BCP 847-48.

6. Those who have studied constitutional law will recognize that the three positions that follow correspond to the basic starting points in jurisprudence.

7. See Amos 1:3–2:5. See also John Barton's comments in *Ethics and the Old Testament* (Harrisburg, Penn.: Trinity Press International, 1998), 58-76.

8. Richard Hooker, *Laws of Ecclesiastical Polity*, 5th ed., vol. 1, bk.1, ch. 8.3, ed. John Keble (Oxford: Clarendon Press, 1865), 226.

～ **Chapter 3: The Book of Nature**

1. "The Sovereignty of Good Over Other Concepts" in Iris Murdoch, *The Sovereignty of Good* (New York: Schocken Books, 1971), 84.

2. Ibid., 78-80.

3. Hymn 409 in *The Hymnal 1982*. Joseph Addison (1672-1719) was an essayist, poet, and statesman.

4. Ibid., Hymn 431 by the contemporary writer Timothy Dudley-Smith (1926–).

5. Ibid., Hymn 372.

6. Richard Hooker, *Laws of Ecclesiastical Polity*, vol. 1, 226.

7. Samuel Taylor Coleridge, "Frost at Midnight," *Selected Poetry and Prose of Coleridge*, ed. Donald A. Stauffer (New York: The Modern Library, 1951), 64.

8. John Keble, *The Christian Year* (London: The Church Literature Association, 1977), 29, 37.

9. *The Declaration of Independence and The Constitution of the United States of America* (Washington, D.C.: Georgetown University Press, 1984), 5-6.

10. *The New York Times*, September 2, 1992.

11. William Temple, *Nature, Man, and God* (London: Macmillan, 1935), 111.

12. Keith Ward, *The Divine Image: The Foundations of Christian Morality* (London: SPCK, 1976), 11.

13. It is worth noting that "chaos theory" works with the assumption of stable patterns within which a tendency to randomness and variability occurs. Thus attention to the variability should not obscure acknowledgment of the pattern.

～ Chapter 4: The Book of Scripture

1. If you find that you wish to pursue issues having to do with the interpretation of scripture you will want to become familiar with volumes two and three in the New Church's Teaching Series, *Opening the Bible* and *Engaging the Word*. These books also identify other resources that will help you to explore some of the issues that arise in connection with scripture and moral theology.

2. This idea of a synthesis between pairs of terms that belong together is emphasized by Martin Thornton as a particularly Anglican virtue in *English Spirituality* (Cambridge, Mass.: Cowley Publications, 1986).

3. For further reading on this topic, see p. 187.

4. These words are found in the solemn declarations made by those who are about to be ordained bishop, priest, or deacon (BCP 513, 526, 538).

5. See Servais Pinckaers, OP, *The Sources of Christian Ethics*, trans. Sr. Mary Thomas Noble, OP (Washington, D.C.: The Catholic University of America Press, 1995), 142. Pinckaers refers to St. Augustine's commentary on the Sermon on the Mount.

6. I am indebted to my colleague, Thomas Osterfield, for the idea of using a mirror, a bookend, and a map as sermon and teaching aids to enhance the point made here.

7. See the section of the Catechism titled, "The Holy Scriptures," from which the central words of this sentence derive (BCP 853-54).

8. *The Hymnal 1982*, Hymn 370, verse 6, attributed to Patrick (372-466).

∿ **Chapter 5: Laws, Manners, and Moral Principles**

1. Judith Martin, *Miss Manners' Guide for the Turn of the Millennium* (New York: Pharos Books, 1989), 13-14.

2. *The New York Times*, January 29, 1999.

3. H. Jackson Brown, Jr., *Life's Little Instruction Book* (Nashville: Rutledge Hill Press, 1991).

4. Geoffrey Rowell, Bishop of Basingstoke, who previously taught at Oxford University.

5. Philip K. Howard, *The Death of Common Sense: How Law is Suffocating America* (New York: Random House, 1994).

∿ **Chapter 6: Sin, Character, and Conscience**

1. See Alistair C. McGrath, "Sin and Salvation" in *The New Dictionary of Christian Ethics and Pastoral Theology* (Leicester and Downers Grove, Ill.: InterVarsity Press, 1995), 28.

2. See the distinction between the sins that exclude us from the kingdom of God (1 Corinthians 6:9-10; Galatians 5:19-21; Ephesians 5:5) and those that do not (James 3:2; 1 John 1:8, 5:16). See also John Macquarrie and James Childress, "Sin(s)" in *The Westminster Dictionary of Christian Ethics* (Philadelphia: Westminster Press, 1986), 585-86.

3. One of the most helpful presentations of the virtues can be found in a little book by Joseph Pieper, who credits Thomas Aquinas with expressing an image of the human person that links the four natural and three theological virtues with true human fulfillment.

See Joseph Pieper, *A Brief Reader on the Virtues of the Human Heart*, trans. Paul C. Duggan (San Francisco: Ignatius Press, 1991).

4. William S. Stafford, *Disordered Loves: Healing the Seven Deadly Sins* (Cambridge, Mass.: Cowley Publications, 1994), 14.

5. Classic texts like F. P. Harton's *The Elements of the Spiritual Life: A Study in Ascetical Theology* (London: SPCK, 1932, 1960) illustrate how moral theology and ascetical theology often overlap, as does Martin Thornton's *English Sprituality: An Outline of Ascetical Theology According to the English Pastoral Tradition* (Cambridge, Mass.: Cowley Publications, 1963, 1986).

6. *Pinocchio*, The Walt Disney Company, Walt Disney Home Video, 88 min., dist. Buena Vista Home Video.

7. Technically, of course, compasses point to what is called magnetic north.

~ **Chapter 7: Love in Acts, Rules, and Principles**

1. For further insight about the concepts described here, see Lindsay Dewar, *An Outline of Anglican Moral Theology* (London: Mowbray, 1968), chapter 3. In relation to the distinctions between modes of casuistry, it is worth noting the view of Kenneth Kirk, who is often credited with inspiring a twentieth-century renewal in the Anglican moral tradition. Kirk, like other Anglican moralists such as Lindsay Dewar, contends that the approach which favors the more probable view is characteristic of the moral theology of the Reformers, and of Anglicans generally. By contrast, Kirk himself inclined toward allowing the *merely probable* approach as providing a better opportunity for moral reasoning to address difficult or uncertain cases, particularly those raised by modern developments in ethics and the sciences. See David Smith's

introduction to a new edition of Kirk's *Conscience and Its Problems: An Introduciton to Casuistry* (Louisville: Westminster John Knox Press, 1999), xii–xxxiii, and Kirk's comments on p. 264, and surrounding, in the same volume.

2. See Thomas Aquinas, *Summa Theologica* I–II.94.4. As quoted in Peter Kreeft's, *Summa of the Summa: The Essential Philosophical Passages of St. Thomas Aquinas' Summa Theologica Edited and Explained for Beginners* (San Francisco: Ignatius Press, 1990), 518: "The practical reason...is busied with contingent matters, about which human actions are concerned: and consequently, although there is necessity in the general principles, the more we descend to matters of detail, the more frequently we encounter defects."

3. Nathaniel Hawthorne, *The Scarlet Letter* (New York: Penguin, 1986), 49. See Hawthorne's description of the scene on pp. 47–55, and the comment made about the leniency of the magistrates on p. 58.

~ **Chapter 8: Building a Case in Christian Ethics**

1. *Resolutions of the Twelve Lambeth Conferences 1867–1988*, ed. Roger Coleman (Toronto: Anglican Book Centre, 1992), 75. No survey of historical and contemporary Christian thought would be complete without references to Roman Catholic papal encyclicals. Further, statements and reports from the Lutheran, Reformed, Methodist, and other Protestant traditions can be instructive, along with those from The World Council of Churches. The clergy and libraries of area churches can help provide copies of these resources.

Resources

Those who wish to pursue further reading in the general field of Christian ethics and moral theology will find a number of helpful books. I would encourage readers who are new to the field to pursue works of general interest first before moving on to consider specific ethical questions because when our attention is focused on controversial matters, we often lose sight of important questions of overall approach and method.

For this reason, I would recommend two basic reference books as a starting point. *The Westminster Dictionary of Christian Ethics*, edited by John Macquarrie and James Childress (Westminster, 1986), is a standard source to be found on many parish and diocesan library shelves. The volume contains a range of articles, from general ones such as Thomas Wood's on "Anglican Moral Theology/Ethics," to more specific treatments of topics such as "Casuistry" in an article by Albert R. Jonsen.

A more recent book of this type that reflects a bit more of a British and international perspective is *The New Dictionary of Christian Ethics and Pastoral Theology*, edited by David J. Atkinson, David F. Field, Arthur Holmes, and Oliver O'Donovan (InterVarsity, 1995). This reference work is comprised of two main sections, the first a series of primary essays on larger themes such as "Love," "Justice and Peace," "History of Christian Ethics," and "Christian Moral Reasoning." The other main section contains shorter articles on topics such as "Health and Health Care," "Jubilee," "Natural Law," and "Sexism."

Both the *Westminster Dictionary* and the *New Dictionary* have articles on the ethics of denominational traditions and on that of individual theologians. For example, the reader will find "Lutheran Ethics" in the *Westminster Dictionary*, and "Martin Luther King" in the *New Dictionary*.

～ Classic Anglican Texts

The classic Anglican introductions to moral theology have been out of print for years. Kenneth Kirk's many books, among them *The Vision of God* (Longmans, Green, 1931) and *Some Principles of Moral Theology* (Longmans, Green, 1920, reprinted 1954), have been used in Episcopal seminaries as source texts for several generations. Readers may also be interested in a new edition of Kenneth Kirk's *Conscience and Its Problems*, edited by David Smith (Westminster/John Knox, 1999). More recent books by authors closely associated with Kirk's work and influence are Robert Mortimer's *The Elements of Moral Theology* (Adam and Charles Black, 1947); Herbert Waddams' *A New Introduction to Moral Theology* (SCM Press, 1965); and Lindsay Dewar's *An Outline of Anglican Moral Theology* (A. R. Mowbray, 1968).

Another Anglican writer whose work is influential was H. R. McAdoo, Archbishop of Dublin and Primate of Ireland. *The Structure of Caroline Moral Theology* (Longmans, Green, 1949) presents a unified vision of Anglican moral theology rooted in the thought of several key figures from the seventeenth century, most notably Robert Sanderson, Jeremy Taylor, and Joseph Hall. Another book that makes reference to the work of particular Caroline theologians is Thomas Wood's *English Casuistical Divinity During the Seventeenth Century* (SPCK, 1952).

A contemporary collection of essays by Anglican ethicists such as Timothy Sedgwick, Harmon Smith, and others is Paul Elmen's *The Anglican Moral Choice* (Morehouse-Barlow, 1983). A new doctoral thesis by Jeffrey Greenman is entitled "Conscience and Contentment: A Reassessment of Seventeenth-Century Anglican Practical Divinity," (Ph.D. dissertation, University of Virginia, 1998). This work helps alert us to the fact that our moral tradition may not be as internally consistent as has been thought.

~ Contemporary Contributions to Anglican Ethics

C. S. Lewis, known primarily as an author of fiction and scholar of English literature, nevertheless wrote a number of books that continue to be helpful to Christian readers. *The Abolition of Man* (Touchstone, 1996) remains important for our consideration of the question of nature and our doctrine of the human person in ethics.

A number of books represent something of the increasingly evident variety of approaches that may be found among the works of contemporary Anglican moral theologians. Readers may wish to look at the following books (alphabetically, by author): Michael Banner, *Christian Ethics and Contemporary Moral Problems* (Cambridge, 1999); Michael Keeling, *The Foundations of Christian Ethics* (T & T Clark, 1990); Oliver O'Donovan, *Resurrection and Moral Order: An Outline for Evangelical Ethics*, 2d ed. (Eerdmans, 1994); Timothy Sedgwick, *The Christian Moral Life: Practices of Piety* (Eerdmans, 1999) and *Sacramental Ethics: Paschal Identity and the Christian Life* (Fortress, 1987); Harmon L. Smith, *Where Two or Three Are Gathered Together: Liturgy and the Moral Life* (Pilgrim, 1995); and William S. Stafford, *Disordered Loves: Healing the Seven Deadly Sins* (Cowley, 1994).

Anglican resources that examine specific moral questions are Robin Gill, *A Textbook of Christian Ethics* (T & T Clark, 1986); Robert E. Hood, *Social Teachings in the Episcopal Church: A Source Book* (Morehouse, 1990); and Timothy F. Sedgwick and Philip Turner, *The Crisis in Moral Teaching in the Episcopal Church* (Morehouse, 1992). In addition, readers may wish to consult the various editions of the *Journal of the General Convention*, published every three years; *Resolutions of the Twelve Lambeth Conferences 1867-1988*, edited by Roger Coleman (Anglican Book Centre, 1992); and *The Official Report of the Lambeth Conference 1998* (Morehouse, 1999).

～ Resources in Christian Ethics from Other Traditions

There are a number of important books and resources that Anglicans will want to be familiar with when they are seeking resources for doing moral theology. A very helpful text that may serve as a comparative reference point is the *Catechism of the Catholic Church*, part 3, "Life in Christ" (Liguori, 1994). In addition, John Paul II's encyclical letter *Veritatis Splendor* (United States Catholic Conference, 1993) can be a helpful stimulant to a discussion about the foundations of a contemporary moral theology. Concerning the virtues, a good introduction is provided by Joseph Pieper's *A Brief Reader on the Virtues of the Human Heart*, translated by Paul C. Duggan (Ignatius Press, 1991).

Two books that provide some history of the Christian ethical tradition as well as contemporary analysis are Stanley Grenz, *The Moral Quest: Foundations of Christian Ethics* (InterVarsity, 1997) and Servais Pinckaers, OP, *The Sources of Christian Ethics*, trans. Sr. Mary Thomas Noble, OP (Catholic University of America, 1995).

An important contribution to the methodology of using scripture in ethics is Richard Hays's *The Moral Vision of the New Testament: A Contemporary Introduction to New Testament Ethics* (Harper, 1996). A helpful resource that also discusses specific ethical issues is Rodger Charles, SJ and Drostan MacLaren, OP, *The Social Teaching of Vatican II: Its Origin and Development* (Ignatius, 1982).

Questions for Group Discussion

~ **Chapter 1: The Walk From the Font**

1. In this chapter, the author describes the moral life as part of our response to the saving mystery we encounter in baptism. In your view, what difference does baptism make for how we actually live our lives? What kind of difference should it make?

2. How do you perceive the relationship between ethics and spirituality, between holiness and righteousness? What connections between these aspects of our faith experience do you make in your own life?

3. Holmgren states that moral theology and pastoral care need to be distinguished in order that each approach to the Christian life will have its own integrity. What is your view of the relationship between moral theology and pastoral care?

~ **Chapter 2: Seeking to Live a Good Life**

1. In this chapter, the author identifies three possible foundations for our notion of the moral good: that which is found in nature, received from history, or

made by convention or choice. Which of these three foundations do you tend to find most persuasive? On which do you tend to rely most often?

2. What difference does referring to salvation history make to our consideration of ethical issues? When talking about aspects of the moral life, in what way can it help us to think in terms of God's intentions for creation, the effects of the fall, or God's purposes in redemption?

3. The author suggests that a demonstrated consensus for a particular view can be a source of assurance when we are thinking about how to respond to an ethical issue. How do you perceive the role of consensus in Anglican theology or morals?

⌒ **Chapter 3: The Book of Nature**
1. Holmgren presents the idea that moral theology works with two primary reference points, the order of creation and our experience of life together within it, as well as scripture and the tradition of reasoned reflection upon it. How do you understand the relationship between these two sources for moral theology?

2. It is quite common to think and say that people have values. What does it mean to say that actions and even objects "have" moral value? In your view, do things like pornographic magazines, hallucinogenic drugs made for street sale, or assault weapons designed for non-military use have moral value that is "there" for us to notice? Or is it simply the way that we use these things that gives them moral value?

3. In your view, what moral principles can we learn from life together in this world, quite aside from those

that scripture teaches us? What are we saying if we claim that non-Christians, even non-religious persons, know some true moral principles as a result of their experience of daily life?

∼ **Chapter 4: The Book of Scripture**
1. What does it mean to distinguish saving knowledge from moral knowledge? For what reasons would we make this distinction when reflecting about moral theology?

2. Holmgren presents two ways that Jesus makes a difference to our ethics: the Jesus whom we meet in scripture, and the Christ in whom we live in the church. In what ways does the Jesus we meet in scripture make a difference to our moral theology? Can you think of other ways than those the author described?

3. In what ways does the Christ in whom we live in the church make a difference to our ethics? What point does the author want to make in saying that our ethics are God-enabled, Christ-indwelled, and Spirit-led?

4. What aspects of the moral teaching found in the Bible are most meaningful or helpful to you? What aspects challenge you the most?

∼ **Chapter 5: Laws, Manners, and Moral Principles**
1. In this chapter, the author presents some of the ways in which laws, manners, and moral principles both overlap and can be distinguished. Can you think of an example of when you have thought about the way they diverge from one another?

2. In what basic way can we say that moral principles stand apart from both laws and manners? What does the author say about the relationship between moral principles and church canons or administrative policies? How do you perceive the relationship between them?

3. Holmgren makes a distinction between describing and telling when talking about moral principles. He suggests that commending the moral good is much more effective than commanding it. Why is this? Does this ring true with your experience?

4. Why should we hesitate about presenting our moral theology in terms of moral codes? What can be an unintended effect of communicating our moral principles in this way?

∽ **Chapter 6: Sin, Character, and Conscience**
1. Holmgren presents acts and character as having a reciprocal relationship, each influencing the other. He also suggests that this is true between individuals and communities. In what ways do our private actions have implications for the communities that we are a part of? Does what I do at work have implications for my parish, and vice versa?

2. Following the example of early Christians in their approach to the preparation of adults for baptism, are there any professions in contemporary life that we might suggest baptismal candidates consider leaving? Are there aspects of your work or profession that seem inconsistent with your faith commitments?

3. Try drawing a "map of the soul." How does your way of picturing the relationship between facets of

our conscious experience compare with those of others in the group?

4. Holmgren presents several common models for thinking about conscience: as an advisor like Jiminy Cricket, as a source of guidance like a compass, and as a reservoir of accumulated conditioning and teaching. What model does the author suggest that we use instead, and why?

⮜ Chapter 7: Love in Acts, Rules, and Principles

1. The author tells a story about starting a food bank in connection with the observation that love may often involve setting conditions in our relationships with others. In what way do you find that love has rules in your relationships or activities?

2. What is your view of how conscience typically functions? What does Holmgren mean when he says that conscience has a role in relation to generic moral principles as well as to particular situations? Why is it sometimes problematic for a person to ask another, "What should I do in this situation?"

3. What suggestions does the author make for how we might address the perception that there is a divergence between the moral teaching of our church and the way that many of us actually live? How do you view the gap between church teaching and moral conduct?

4. Who, if anyone, determines the meaning of our actions? How do you regard the role of judgment in the discernment of moral acts?

~ Chapter 8: Building a Case in Christian Ethics

1. At several points in this book, Holmgren has said that Anglicans have no standard rule book or official compendium of moral teachings. Where does he suggest that we will find dependable moral principles with which to shape our lives and respond to moral issues?

2. In describing the process of identifying biblical texts that may be relevant for considering an ethical question, the author suggests that a parish study group brainstorm together to create a list. Using a newsprint pad, what kind of a list can you come up with?

3. What resources does your parish have that can help you build a case in responding to an ethical question or issue?

4. Throughout the book, the author has quoted portions of hymns and texts from *The Book of Common Prayer* that have significance for reflection about the moral life. Are there similar passages that you find helpful and meaningful?